Praise for *Dancing With*

"An extraordinary collect[ion] [...] front lines of global infrastructure finance. Mitch Silk and Seth Tan, two leading practitioners of infrastructure finance over the past 30 years, illuminate the essential role of private investment in meeting the world's energy needs."
– *Andrés Gluski, President and CEO, The AES Corporation*

"*Dancing With Giants* takes readers inside some of the biggest infrastructure deals of the last several decades and you'll return with several important lessons learned."
– *Graham Vinter, Chair, Global Project Development and Finance Practice, Covington & Burling LLP*

"Written by the people who did the deals, a superb and engaging account of the rise, and sometimes fall, of infrastructure projects in Asia and America since the 1980s."
– *Ashley C. Wilkins, former Head of Project Finance and Advisory, SocGen Asia*

"*Dancing With Giants* uses engaging vignettes and market trends to provide a thoughtful dive into the legal, political, and financial intricacies of international infrastructure finance."
– *Philip Wood CBE QC Hon, author of the nine volumes in the series the Law and Practice of International Finance, Yorke Distinguished Visiting Fellow at the University of Cambridge*

"Insights from the past 30 years of infrastructure development in Asia present many important learnings for infrastructure today and tomorrow. The alternating stories between Seth and Mitch as they dance with the Giants makes it an interesting read."
– *Lim Chze Cheen, Director and Head, ASEAN Connectivity Division, ASEAN Secretariat*

More Praise for *Dancing With Giants*

"Governments used to build and operate infrastructure. But this is not true anymore. We now need to rely more on the private sector to build and operate infrastructure around the world. Seth is one of few with extensive experience structuring and financing infrastructure projects in Asia in the private sector who joined a government organization to play a key role in setting a new direction. This book is very unique and I learned a lot from reading it."
– *Keiko Honda, Adjunct Senior Research Scholar and Adjunct Professor, Columbia University*

"Mitch Silk and Seth Tan artfully use the market developments and stories in *Dancing With Giants* to illustrate the importance of infrastructure finance to global growth. They also provide a timely reminder of what the word infrastructure really means and its power to advance human dignity and quality of life."
– *J. Steven Dowd, Former U.S. Executive Director, European Bank of Reconstruction and Development, and African Development Bank.*

"Two lifetimes worth of rich battle experiences on this sometimes hair-tearing subject of Project Finance."
– *Pang Yee Ean, CEO Surbana Jurong Capital*

"A thoroughly enjoyable personal account of the global energy and infrastructure journey that many of us have taken, which evokes many great memories while highlighting many important lessons learned along the way. "
– *Nicholas Wong, Global Co-Head Worldwide Projects Group and Co-Head Global Financial Markets, Asia Pacific at Clifford Chance*

"Infrastructure in the next 30 years may be very different from today or not yet exist as needs will change and technology advancement can offer new solutions. But the past can offer good principles to follow for future development. It is great to read about two practitioners, Mitch and Seth, who have lived and breathed infrastructure in the last 30 years."

– Marie Lam-Frendo, CEO, Global Infrastructure Hub
  (a G20 initiative)

"Growth in energy and infrastructure is essential to prosperity and access in Latin America and throughout the world. *Dancing With Giants* makes a fantastic case for the importance of the private sector, governments, and communities to work together on infrastructure projects that can improve the world."

– Eliot Pedrosa, Immediate Past U.S. Executive Director, Inter-
  America Development Bank

"Mitch Silk is a leading infrastructure finance expert. He and Seth Tan bring to light the challenges and rewards of growth through infrastructure finance with flair and insight in their book *Dancing With Giants*. It was a great read."

– Jacob Worenklein, Former Chairman of Ravenswood Power
  and the largest power plant in New York City.

"*Dancing With Giants* is a riveting firsthand account of project finance and infrastructure in a world of increasingly interconnected economies and governments. The authors demonstrate why infrastructure, and power projects in particular, are such important factors in global development, with lessons for the future. Well worth a read for any practitioner or development professional."

– DJ Norquist, U.S. Executive Director,
  World Bank Group (2019-2021)

Edited and Produced by Raab & Co. | raabandco.com

RAAB&Co

Designed by Andrew Bell | andrewbelldesigns.co.uk
Cover Photo by Billy Hustace
Image credits on p. 135 are an extension of the copyright page.

First Paperback Edition
10 9 8 7 6 5 4 3 2 1

ISBN: 978-1-7331334-7-0

Printed in the United States

A Lawyer and Banker Share Their
Passion for Infrastructure Finance

DANCING

WITH

GIANTS

MITCHELL A. SILK & SETH TAN

CONTENTS

PROLOGUE

What could a U.S. lawyer and a Singaporean banker possibly have in common?

Well, our paths first crossed in the late 1990s when each of us was supporting a different bidder for a water treatment plant in Chengdu, China. The project was based on a Build-Operate-Transfer (BOT) structure, under which a developer with know-how and financing builds the plant, gets it up and running, and then transfers it to a domestic owner or government at the end of an agreed operating period. BOT projects are an example of one of many public-private partnership approaches that governments use to attract international private sector investment for their infrastructure projects. These projects usually last for 20 or more years—long enough to amortize debt and allow the investor to earn back its capital investment and make a profit. In the case of Chengdu, both of our clients lost the bid, though Mitch ended up representing the lenders in the financing of the project.

Two decades later, our paths crossed again. This time, we were working for our respective governments. Mitch joined the senior leadership at the U.S. Department of the Treasury in 2017 as Deputy Assistant Secretary for Infrastructure, Energy and Investment. He was later appointed by the President and confirmed by the Senate as Assistant Secretary for International Markets. At roughly the same time, Seth took a position as Executive Director of Infrastructure Asia, a regional infrastructure facilitation office under the Singapore Government.

Mitch designed and implemented the signature U.S. whole-of-government infrastructure finance initiative which assisted

40 foreign partners in attracting private investment for growth of their energy and infrastructure sectors. Seth was engaged in a similar pursuit to help mobilize more private sector participation in South and Southeast Asian infrastructure. We were both key interlocutors for our respective governments in the implementation of the bilateral international arrangement between the U.S. and Singapore governments, known as the Framework to Strengthen Infrastructure Finance and Market Building Cooperation, signed on October 16, 2019.

Dancing With Giants is a series of alternating stories that takes a canter through the rise and fall of giants in the form of markets, players, risk mitigation approaches, and financing tools and structures, including the important approach called Project Financing, in the field defined broadly as Infrastructure Finance.

In this book, we're going to tell stories about our careers and the projects we have worked on. But this is more than just a storybook. We'll be tracing the evolution of infrastructure finance, with a focus on Asia. More specifically, we will describe how limited recourse project finance tools, solutions, and structures were used to meet the giant demands for energy and infrastructure development and financing to fuel economic growth.

It all began with the application of these concepts to meet, for example, financing needs for the emergence of independent power in the United States, as well as offshore oil development in the North Sea. We'll begin our story in the Stone Age—fax machines, telex, and trains with hard seats. In the late 1980s and early 1990s, emerging markets started to open up to foreign investment in energy and infrastructure. Foreign developers and their financiers began to "export" these project structuring and financing approaches into their projects in the emerging markets in Asia and elsewhere. Giant infrastructure growth in the emerging markets followed in fits and spurts.

Then we'll explore how market standards emerged around these projects on which the whole region's international infrastructure finance markets operated and grew, with variances by country. We'll show how a matured and established market standard empowered local equipment suppliers, developers, and banks in those emerging markets to finance and spearhead projects on their own. And we will illustrate the consequences of skating too close to or over the edge of the market standard.

The best measure of an emerging market succeeding in establishing its own set of market standards and depth in its own markets is when it stands on its own feet. We'll explore how participants who readily adopted these standards matured, stood on their feet, and began to spread their wings abroad by exporting their own knowhow, financing, and technology throughout the world.

After years working in Asia, Mitch came back to the U.S. (see Chapter 5) to find the U.S. infrastructure market undergoing a sea of change. He describes this new infrastructure landscape, and explains how sound fundamentals in development and finance in all markets—emerging and developed—are paramount to success.

Finally, against this interesting historical backdrop, we'll both explore what the future of infrastructure and infrastructure finance might look like.

We were front and center for almost three decades as this industry went through immense change and growth—whether it was transition from telex to high-speed internet communications or from coal-fired power plants to renewables. It was an extraordinary run, and the excitement and the challenge is what kept us in the game.

Why Infrastructure?

We both found ourselves in the same industry for different reasons. Mitch, in part whimsical and in part philosophical, attributes his first break of securing a job at a leading project finance firm his "vast" experience in power generation—he had been dutifully paying his utility bill to ConEd for years prior to the job interview! And since then, his projects have enabled him to continue paying the bills, and then some.

For Seth, ever the pragmatist, there seemed to always be a need for bankers on essential infrastructure projects, even during crises like the Asian Financial Crisis in 1997. While it was very painful working on restructuring in the aftermath of a crisis, it was still work that put bread on the table and he learned a lot from navigating the ups and downs of the market.

But it was really our passion for the impact and complexity of the field that kept us involved. The projects were giants, the players were giants and, most of all, the problem solving produced giant headaches given the myriad challenges involved with structuring, documenting, and negotiating a successful project.

What can we say? We both like dancing with giants.

An Industry Like No Other

Infrastructure is a giant's business—giant markets, giant companies, giant budgets, giant complexities, giant timelines, giant risks, giant challenges, and, of course, giant headaches. It's endlessly fascinating to dance with these massive entities, to watch them dance, to get them to say "yes," and to watch how they get others to say "yes." Over time, we watched some infrastructure sectors—such as renewable energy—grow into gargantuan giants themselves. It was eye-opening to see how these giants evolved and survived or fell behind and failed. The name of the game was to formulate elegant and equitable approaches to manage the gigantic risks presented.

We both got started in the infrastructure sector at the right time. Working on infrastructure in the 1990s was exhilarating. We both worked on many first-of-their-kind projects that required a fresh look at novel structures with complex commercial, financial, and legal concerns; engagements with multiple counterparties; and a ton of time convincing everyone involved. Many of the projects were the largest in the world at the time in terms of size, but even the small ones—and sometimes particularly the small ones—presented idiosyncrasies and challenges disproportionately larger than their size. Every deal was a new puzzle waiting to be solved. For both of us, solving the puzzle meant we'd be allowed to keep playing the game we loved. Sometimes projects would take years to finalize, discussions would proceed with fits and spurts. Yet other projects would suffer protracted delays before finishing smoothly. Delays could be due to political cycles or changes in policy or market disruption, and it was all beyond the control of lawyers and bankers. We have learned the most from the projects that failed, but the drive to succeed and close projects is most certainly what kept us motivated. At the end of the day, the market measures success by closed deals and so we always remained laser focused on getting projects across the line and to closing.

Looking back at the last three decades of work, we've seen the giants change with the seasons. New giants don't always dance well from the get-go, and, as we both learned one way or another, giants don't always get their way. There is a certain rhythm to infrastructure, and the success of an infrastructure project requires its own set of right conditions.

This book is based on our experiences. As such, it is by definition limited in scope and coverage. This is not an exhaustive treatment of project finance or investment in global infrastructure by any means. Nonetheless, the issues identified and lessons learned are representative of general practices in our field.

What Is Project Financing?

In the world of infrastructure, project financing is more than just a project that needs financing. Indeed, describing "Project Finance" has become the subject of many learned tomes, including works by some of the best project finance experts in the world.[1] One

---

1   Mitch's former partner at Allen & Overy Philip Wood published in 1980 one of the earliest monographs on the topic, titled *The Law and Practice of International Finance*, which had a chapter on project finance. That volume grew from one volume to six in 1995, seven in 2007, and nine in 2019, containing a total of three million words and volumes dedicated to specific project finance topics.

of Mitch's former partners, Graham Vinter, uses the following definition in his seminal volume *Project Finance:*[2]

> "Project finance is financing the development or exploitation of a right, natural resource or other asset where the bulk of the financing is not to be provided by any form of share capital and is to be paid principally out of revenues produced by the project in question."

In layman's terms, a bank invests significant debt, sometimes as much as 70% of total project cost, alongside the equity investors and then relies on repayment based on the project's cash flow. As you can imagine, a lot can go wrong! The key elements distilled from this definition have guided our approaches as professionals and government officials.

First, long-term project contracts serve as the foundation of project financing because they provide the basis for a predictable long-term revenue stream, a firm project budget, and protections against cost overruns.

Second, the contracts must allocate risk to the party best suited to control a particular risk. Banks have limited recourse mainly to the project's assets, and typically not the shareholders. If the project does not perform, it is highly important that they understand the risks that a project may face over the life of the loan (often over 10 years). Once the lenders understand these risks through detailed analysis and due diligence, they must allocate those risks as equitably as possible and ensure there is no ambiguity about who is responsible for what. Precise legal structuring and drafting therefore become paramount.

Both of us witnessed how these basic principles underpinned every contract and were eventually adopted as general accepted

---

2 Graham Vinter built Allen & Overy's global project finance practice. He published the leading treatise on the legal aspect of project finance, entitled, not surprisingly, *Project Finance*, in 1995. This volume has been reprinted and expanded three times, with the fourth edition appearing in 2013.

project finance standards—what we call a market standard. We watched the market standard develop in emerging countries like China as they improved their domestic infrastructure and pushed for outbound investment in the 2000s, as well as in developed countries like the U.S. as they sought to achieve energy independence and a strong renewables industry.

Project Finance is in many ways the art of documentation— documenting risk, documenting projections, documenting mutual understandings, documenting ambiguities, and documenting promises. For example, Seth once had a three-hour negotiation on the word "solely" as it applied to various situations. The sponsor wanted to ensure if something bad happened, they would only be responsible for making good some payments if the event was "solely" caused by them.

Having spent our lives in infrastructure, we seek to highlight in the core chapters of this book some lessons for future bankers and lawyers in similar positions. In the final chapter, we explore how to lay a solid foundation for the future of infrastructure at a time when the rapid growth that we see is subject to impact by major unknowns and variables like the advent of disruptive technology, the COVID-19 pandemic, and the emergence of transitional energy and infrastructure. Interesting and challenging times indeed. Fasten your seatbelts.

CHAPTER 1

THE STONE AGE OF PROJECT FINANCING

By Mitchell A. Silk

n 1986, I had just graduated law school and served as an intern in the Beijing Office of the Coudert Brothers—one of the earliest truly international law firms—as a practical training part of a U.S. Government fellowship to China. This position afforded me a unique vantage point to witness the structuring, documentation, and negotiation of project financing of the An Tai Bao Coal Mining Project.

At the time, An Tai Bao was the world's largest open-pit coal mine and a pet project of the late Dr. Armand Hammer, then Chairman of Occidental Petroleum Corporation. Dr. Hammer developed and financed the project through Oxy Coal Mine Island Creek of China Coal, a joint venture between his Occidental Petroleum Corporation and various subsidiaries of the Chinese Ministry of Coal. Joint ventures were new to China and project financing was unprecedented. This was the first time that these foreign concepts were being tried and tested in China on such a large scale.

My host institution was the International Law Institute at Beijing University. I stayed in the foreigners' dormitory called Shao Yuan, which comprised three Soviet-style buildings with double bedrooms and communal toilets and showers. Accommodations were sparse and rudimentary. Every week the winds from the Gobi Desert left an inch of dust on the windowsills. It was from this vantage point, at 25 years old, that I started my career in project finance.

I was excited and nervous: just out of law school and already working on a US$675 million project. That was a lot of money in those days—equivalent to US$1.63 billion in 2021. It was the first giant, limited recourse international project financing ever completed in China. There was no precedent to speak of—this was literally the first time that many of the documents and concepts integral to the financing were being tried and tested in China. It was an exceptionally instructive case study for my fellowship work.

The success of the project was attributable in no small part to the expert lawyers behind it. My direct supervisors Owen Nee and Peter Cleary, partners in the Hong Kong office of Coudert Brothers, were the lead lawyers for Oxy's interests.[3] Owen was one of the earliest pioneers representing foreign investors in China, and became one of the few experts of joint ventures and similar transactions. Peter was a lawyer's lawyer and became recognized as one of the leading project finance lawyers in Asia. Owen drafted and negotiated the project documents—the joint venture contract, various contracts for the construction and expansion of the mine and its operation, and the offtake agreements for the coal. Peter was counsel for the borrower in the financing and documented and closed the main finance and security documents.

A syndicate led by Bank of America, the Royal Bank of Canada, the Industrial Bank of Japan, Crédit Lyonnais, and Bank of China arranged the US$475 million loan, with 34 consortium banks in the syndicate. With virtually no statutory guidance or practice, the financiers settled on a fairly sophisticated security structure covering both assets and contract rights and supported by various limited guarantees to get the financing across the line.

One of my tasks was to ensure that the local Chinese law counsel to the borrower issued an opinion that would support the requirements of the financing. Boy, was that a doozy! We were ably assisted by Wei Jiaju and Chen Zhuping of the China Legal Consultancy Center, a captive law firm under the Ministry of Justice, which meant that their work was guided by novel legal concepts as well as the Chinese Communist Party. The fact

---

3 Sadly, they both passed away in early 2021, long before their time.

that there was so little policy guidance made this negotiation highly challenging.

I refer to this period as the Stone Age of project financing because of the slow and challenging ways in which we documented and negotiated projects at the time, as well as the lack of precedent and legal frameworks to guide us. I guess that made us cavemen.

The Wild, Wild East

A trip to the Coudert Brothers' offices involved a journey crosstown to the Beijing Hotel, usually in a 1950s Soviet sedan. It was around 11 miles and took the better part of an hour. The drive required careful navigation through a sea of bicycles that overtook the road each morning, and the occasional horse-pulled cart. There were maybe two Western-style office buildings in existence then, and the Coudert Brothers' office was actually just a hotel suite converted into a makeshift office. To make matters even more challenging, the project itself was located in Shanxi province. Since China's domestic commercial airline industry was at a very nascent stage, this meant we had to take an eight-hour train journey any time the lawyers were required for meetings at the plant.

While we sometimes sent documents by fax, this limited us to single party transmissions at a time, so we would often deliver documents by hand or snail mail. Certain document transmissions went by telex—a sort of glorified telegram that allows typed transmissions over phone lines. Documents sent via telex had to be entered manually and the transmission speed felt actually slower than a snail's. A telex machine could, with a stable connection, transmit around a word a minute. Of course, we were never blessed with a stable phone line in Beijing so multiple attempts to transmit were the norm. This meant that the transmission of a 10-page, double-spaced document would require 40 minutes in a best-case scenario. While as a lawyer this was a boon for billable hours, it was grating on the nerves and detrimental to productivity. Fax machines cut that time considerably, but it would still take the better part of an hour to transmit a 100-page document, again, assuming a stable phone line. I think you see now why this felt like the Stone Ages to me. My, how times have changed, with the ability to distribute hundreds of pages of legal documents by email in nanoseconds.

Unfortunately, the Oxy coal mine project never realized the economic potential envisioned by Dr. Hammer. The joint venture project had not shown a profit in its first five years of operation, and was plagued with disputes between the joint venture partners. Shortly after Dr. Hammer's death, Occidental Petroleum underwent a major restructuring and shed itself of a number of unprofitable ventures. In June 1991, Occidental sold down its interest in the joint venture to its Chinese partner. Even with the best of structuring and documentation, unfavorable investment environments and politics can get in the way of a well-planned and executed project.

The Great Leap Forward: China's Insatiable Need for Capital

It turns out the adage is right: If you build it, they will come. Or, in the case of infrastructure financing, even if you just *want* to build it, they will come. As such, when China opened to foreign investment in energy and infrastructure in the early 1990s, it represented one of the world's most fertile markets for infrastructure development. The transaction record and projected need for foreign capital were great attractions to developers and financiers seeking higher yields and higher returns than stable markets like the U.S. provided.[4] Every major independent power developer and equipment supplier descended on China. Along with them came the leading project finance lenders, financial advisors, and professional advisors after their business.

---

4   This section references Mitchell Silk's article "Critical Issues in Project Development and Project Finance in China," *Project Finance International*, Issue 146, June 3, 1998, pp. 51-57.

Growth during this period was demonstrable and the demand for capital was gargantuan but unachievable. Between 1979—the year that China ushered in its Open Door policy—and 1995, China completed 87 power projects and utilized just under US$15 billion of foreign capital, with foreign capital representing a mere 10% of total investment in the sector. Given the lack of depth and liquidity in the long-term domestic credit markets at the time in China, Chinese officials projected the need for foreign funds from 1996 to 2000 at not less than US$100 billion—20% of the walloping US$500 billion in infrastructure spending projected that would fund the development of roughly 88,000 MW of installed generating capacity to meet China's development needs.

These were overly optimistic projections. The investment goals represented a transactional volume and velocity that was simply impossible to meet. Were Chinese policymakers to have opened the aperture on foreign participation in a manner more aligned with the fundamental market standards governing risk allocation, the narrative and the results would have been radically different. But they were not. That reality did not, however, dissuade foreign investors who flocked to both China, India and other countries in Asia to exploit opportunities in their power sectors.

The leading China transactions of the time were the 1400 MW Zhuhai Power Project, the 700 MW Laibin B Power Project, and the 100 MW Tangshan Power Project. For some perspective on just how much their projections missed the mark, US$100 billion was the same as over 80 Zhuhai projects, nearly 170 Laibin projects, and almost 600 Tangshan Power Projects. Foreign investment in the sector was, in actuality, a small fraction of what was required. This highlights the difference between policy that encourages foreign investment, and one that merely tolerates it. As we will see in the coming pages, China eventually established a more hospitable investment environment which fostered limited growth for a limited period.

The Emergence of a Standard

This start of foreign investment in energy and infrastructure wasn't dissimilar to the creation of the world: in the beginning there was darkness and confusion.[5] The sheer demand for growth presented seemingly unlimited investment opportunity. However, in actuality, investment activity was relatively flat. There were a lot of investors chasing a ton of deals, but few actually got across the line.

The relatively low level of deal velocity was largely due to the legal and regulatory risks presented in the context of limited-recourse project financing in China. The approval requirements at the development and financing stages were numerous, demanding, time-consuming, and, in some cases, actually impossible. Regulatory risk was challenging for foreign lenders to understand and quantify. Foreign investors and their lenders did not exactly find Chinese regulators to be friendly or accessible. At the time, the Three No Policy (三不政策 *san bu zhengce*) was at the heart of Taiwan's policy toward the mainland: no contact, no negotiation, and no compromise. Many foreign investors felt that their project regulators had their own Three No Policy for every question that the investors had about their projects' development and financing: 不知道 (*bu zhi dao*), 不清楚 (*bu qing chu*) and 不好说 (*bu hao shuo*) ("I don't know," "I'm not clear," and "It's hard to say").

As a result of this darkness and confusion, foreign developers and lenders formulated various "innovative" structures in an attempt to mitigate these risks. However, many of these structures—like splitting projects to avoid planning approvals—presented material enforceability risks and would ultimately derail entire projects that adopted this approach. Investors utilized other more enforceable approaches to create a legal promise of long-term sustainable cash flows—like payment shortfall guarantees. These, however, invariably increased the cost of power or tolls (in the case of road projects) to consumers, and added an additional and unnecessary layer of legal risk.

---

5 *Genesis* 1:2.

After a number of years, the emergence of a "market standard" as well as improved communication technology and infrastructure—in no small part due to the infrastructure projects themselves—took us out of the Stone Age and into the Golden Age of the '90s. The Asian Financial Crisis, however, threatened to derail our blossoming industry, and it was up to lawyers such as myself and bankers such as Seth to fashion a more resilient future for infrastructure financing.

The Other Three No Policy

CHAPTER 2

THE GOLDEN AGE CAME AND WENT

By Seth Tan

I n the 1990s, it seemed like giants could get anything financed. The industry was experiencing tremendous growth which, while exciting, was ultimately not sustained. While most of emerging Asia was just getting their feet wet with project finance, certain countries such as Thailand were establishing policies, laws, and regulations that created an attractive environment for foreign investment in infrastructure. In the early days of my infrastructure finance career, I was working as a project finance analyst for the French bank Paribas. My fondest memories of my early days in project finance were the frequent travel to Asian cities. It took a bit of courage as I often had to jump into taxis where the drivers had little or even no English capability. One time in Bangkok, I showed the taxi driver the business card of the national oil company I had a meeting with. He seemed to understand and drove for 30 minutes, only to arrive not at the head offices, but a gas station with the same logo.

My first transaction was the US$1.5 billion Rayong Refinery in Thailand led by Chase Manhattan Bank. Given its size and complexity, this was a landmark project financing for Thailand, and indeed Southeast Asia on the whole. In the case of the Rayong refinery, the two giant stakeholders—Shell and Petroleum Authority of Thailand (PTT)—strongly supported the project given the forecasted need for huge amounts of refined petroleum products.

Wrong place at the right time.

The Thai infrastructure market was similarly situated to other Southeast Asian markets. There was an insatiable need for capital, which the relatively undeveloped local financing markets were unable to support. In terms of both liquidity and tenors, the local debt market was not deep enough at that time to support project financings of the magnitude of the Rayong project. It was therefore necessary to tap the international bank markets for financing giants to support the project. With the three types of giants— needs, sponsors and financiers—it felt like any infrastructure could be structured as a means to arrange long-term financing. Many infrastructure projects were considered country-critical ("needs"), hence involved giants like top government offices, state-owned enterprises, and multinational corporations.

In the 1990s, project financing was considered one of the more complex types of financing. Emerging Asian economies like Thailand, Indonesia, and the Philippines were leveraging on long-term project financing to build large-scale infrastructure like liquefied natural gas (LNG) terminals, mega power projects, oil refineries, and petrochemical projects needed to support their fast-growing economies. Given the complex structuring, there were only a handful of banks, that could put the financing together. Paribas (which later merged with BNP to become BNP Paribas) was one of them.

When I think about this time in my career and in the industry, I recall the Chinese saying "时势造英雄," which means "the era makes the hero." Well, the 1990s was the era of foreign capital and foreign technology, including project financing skills. Project finance bankers could pat themselves on the back at the end of each year as they secured good fees and multi-year interest income for their banks. Just as important, they could point to tangible and impressive infrastructure they helped enabled. Such was the Golden Era of project finance. If you mastered the "science" and appropriately allocated the risks, long-term limited recourse finance followed and you could stand out as an expert in a burgeoning field.

A Career Fit

I was young and ambitious, but also introverted. I felt that being a project finance banker was the best job in the world. I was neither good-looking nor outspoken, hence did not see myself as a relationship banker. I was not very quick with numbers, hence the trading desk seemed out of the question. But project finance? That was just right. It required long hours and hard work to understand how the myriad of contracts come together to provide long-term project cash-flow stability, and it required building complex cash-flow models capable of surviving many dynamic scenarios. This, I thought, I could do. I must have done reasonably well, as I soon managed to help my bank secure roles where we were even paid additional fees for doing such work. As this was a new field in emerging Asia, few hinterland bankers had yet acquired these skills, so I was flying around a lot. This extensive travel schedule also added to it being the best job I could imagine.

Invisible Risks

For almost a decade, the infrastructure finance industry experienced growth, and an immense number of transactions. Then, in 1997, the Asian Financial Crisis changed all that.

The crisis stress-tested the structuring and risk mitigation approaches that the bankers and lawyers had been developing. While everyone had been eager to make projects as risk-free as possible through complex structuring, it turns out that was simply not possible because there were too many stakeholders and unforeseeable factors to make fully confident promises.

I will discuss a couple of blind spots that the financial crisis revealed, and in the next chapter by Mitch, we'll learn about how addressing the blind spots contributed to a market standard that strengthened the entire industry.

One key blind spot revealed by the financial crisis was the effect of foreign exchange rate fluctuation on transactions. Most large infrastructure projects at that time borrowed long-term USD debt, and project revenue was contractually indexed to USD. This was a seemingly elegant fix on paper because it took care of international lenders' concern that the foreign exchange risk was untenable. By tying project revenues to USD, the risk was "passed on" beyond the project to the offtaker, which was usually supported by the local government.

The political and economic impact of a fully indexed project—a project tied to an international currency—turned out, however, to be considerable when local currencies were devalued. The local governments would either have to find ways to absorb the higher debt cost or risk paying a political price for raising tariffs (in the case of a power project, electricity tariffs) to compensate for the higher costs associated with indexing. This phenomenon was one root cause of the challenges that foreign-invested projects experienced in China in the late 1990s and early 2000s, and Mitch discusses this in Chapter 7.

Looking back at some of the project finance syndication debt information memorandums prior to 1997, I can't help but notice most did not run significant downside sensitivities in regard to exchange rate fluctuations. When the exchange rate deteriorated by more than 200% (in the case of Indonesia, 600%) during the crisis, there was no way the host government could make good the linkage to USD.

When the dust settled, this revelation led to governments focusing on increasing their foreign exchange reserves, as well as strengthening and deepening their local debt markets and approving indexing only on those portions of tariffs where it was absolutely necessary to attract foreign capital.

Another blind spot the crisis revealed was the risk of a domino effect which could needlessly topple a whole project. Some transactions relied on parent company support, not just from a financial perspective but from an operational perspective, such as reliance on the parent's jetty facility, supply of feedstock, or the project was located within the parent company's site. When the parent company also became affected by the crisis, this could create all sorts of issues for every aspect of the project. Addressing this blind spot meant underlining the importance of structuring projects so that the myriad risks were as independent and insulated as possible.

Like many other infrastructure projects, the Rayong Refinery was not spared by the crisis. One of the vital features of the loan had been a sizeable cash pool—elegantly called a cash deficiency support—that the sponsors committed to inject if necessary to address any oil market deterioration. That cash pool was completely drawn in the aftermath of the Financial Crisis but it was still not enough to get the refinery back on its feet. The sponsors decided to enter into an operating alliance with one of its competitors (Caltex Star Refinery), and this allowed both projects to better align their feedstock sourcing, yield more efficiencies, and also reduce some products in response to the reduced market needs.

The Crisis showed that, notwithstanding the rigor and best efforts of bankers, lawyers, technical and financial advisors, project finance is not an exact science as there could be invisible risks that no one predicted.

Getting Back to Basics

After the financial crisis, catchphrases like "getting back to basics," "looking at credit 101," and "looking at fundamentals" became popular among project finance practitioners. It became clear to everyone that it may not be possible to identify all risks nor to fully mitigate them. It became a market standard for project and commercial structure to allow for some uncertainties and some flexibility to address numerous scenarios—rather than trying to be leakproof and still be unable to weather unpredictable market events.

In the ensuing years, you could still find clever sponsors trying to practice project finance as if it were a science. Of course, this often worked to their advantage. Some would work hard to ensure the project's feasibility study and various due diligence reports prepared by third-party consultants checked all the typical boxes for project finance lenders. Some embarked on what I call the "magic of the whiteboard" and de-risked the project on paper to maximize the project finance debt amount. In some dramatic examples, the debt amount put together by the winning bidder was higher than the total enterprise value (debt plus equity) for the second-place bidder. Over the long term, however, these sorts of tactics are not sustainable nor good for the market. By and large, the Asian Financial Crisis taught project finance lenders and project sponsors to be more circumspect and to build more resilient projects rather than trying to completely de-risk.

Having witnessed how projects suffered through the Asian Financial Crisis—including sitting on a Thai lube oil project's debt-restructuring steering committee for over four years—I was also forever changed. It became clear to me that there was not a one-size-fits all project financing approach. Instead, I needed to think more about *financing projects* rather than project *financing*. By that I mean I really needed to drill down to the fingerprint and unique identity of a project and its stakeholders. Only this way could I understand with clarity and realism the project's risks and how well those risks could be mitigated.

The lessons learned during the Asian Financial Crisis by me personally and our industry as a whole contributed to a more sustainable project finance community. As Mitch will discuss in the next chapter, the Financial Crisis also led directly to the emergence of generally accepted and good rules of engagement for infrastructure projects—rules we call the market standard.

CHAPTER 3

THE EMERGENCE OF A MARKET STANDARD

By Mitchell A. Silk

B y the late 1990s, a market standard for foreign energy and infrastructure developers and financiers began to clearly emerge in markets like China and Southeast Asia. A number of major foreign-invested power projects had closed and each of these projects moved the market standard forward. By this time, I had been in project finance for more than a decade and played a role in closing some of these landmark projects. Here follows some inside ball that explains how each of these projects helped develop the market standard as we know it today.

Equitable Risk Allocation in Gansu Province

A key tenet of the market standard is that risk should be allocated as equitably among stakeholders as possible. This was certainly clear in the case of the Gansu Jingyuan Phase 2 Project. I represented the foreign investor Community Energy Alternatives (the independent power subsidiary of the New Jersey utility PSEG) in this 2x300 MW expansion through a Sino-U.S. joint venture of an existing domestic 800 MW power plant. The Gansu Jingyuan Project was the first Sino-U.S. joint venture power plant to fund equity and took the better part of two years to complete in 1996.

It took months to negotiate through basic contractual concepts like a take-or-pay obligation in the power offtake agreement, force majeure protection, and a turnkey, all-in, fixed-price and date-certain construction contract. A contract negotiation session—

almost all of which took place in Gansu's capital of Lanzhou, which at the time had no Western hotels—would typically span over periods of three to five days. We would start at 8 a.m., take a mandatory two-hour lunch break, and finish promptly at 5 p.m. Almost every evening, we would attend a dinner banquet at which our hosts would ply us with Gansu's version of Maotai—a popular, high-grade Chinese distilled alcoholic spirit with an alcohol content usually exceeding 50%. It struck me at the time that these spirits were certainly potent enough to fuel our car.

Our client's Chinese partners were all Government cadres from the Gansu Provincial Government and the Central Government. It was as much a commercial and technical negotiation as it was a political one. We had been negotiating the deal for well over a year with the Gansu Provincial authorities, who held a majority of the Chinese participation in the project alongside one of China's State investment companies. Our partners were well versed in highly technical power sector issues but had not done a transaction with foreign investors or ever dealt with foreign commercial banks.

Up, Up and Away on China Northwest

By the time we were working on the Gansu project in the mid-1990s, the logistics of doing business in China had improved since we worked on the Oxy Coal Mine Project. While we had the benefit of emerging telecommunications and internet technology, it was still a struggle. Large and clunky laptops were cumbersome to lug around and the transmission of documents were wholly a function of the reliability and speed of available phone lines. By way of example, phone lines were so unreliable in Lanzhou that it was almost impossible to transmit a document to a colleague down the hall in the same hotel, let alone to the office in Hong Kong. We therefore still had to rely heavily on offices and business centers in hotels to print documents for negotiations. In addition, transport was still highly challenging. Lanzhou was, in the best case, a five-hour flight from Hong Kong. →

> → If you were lucky, you could find a good enough schedule on one of the major Chinese airlines and fly through Beijing, Shanghai, or Guangzhou. On the upside, you got to fly in a reasonably modern and safe plane. On the downside, the layovers were often nine or ten hours. Frequently, scheduling required flying on China Southwest, one of China's regional carriers with a hub in nearby Xi'an and regular flights to Lanzhou. A flight on China Southwest meant airplane equipment like an old Soviet Tupolev or Ilyushin. Talk about white knuckles while flying!

As luck would have it, a major government restructuring occurred as we were concluding a year of negotiating the project's contracts. As a part of that restructuring, shareholding on the Chinese side of the joint venture shifted, and with that came a dramatic change in negotiating position and style. A newly reorganized State Development & Investment Corporation (SDIC) emerged from the government restructuring. SDIC was tasked with looking after capital investments in domestic projects, and stepped into the shoes of one of the initial Chinese participants in the joint venture with a majority of the Chinese interests. As such, overnight, we were dealing with a new dominant partner at the Central Government level.

Our prior working relations were primarily at the provincial level. With this change in composition of the Chinese shareholders came a distinct difference in approach to negotiation. The provincial parties would not move without the blessing of the SDIC and the newly established SDIC acted more like a government bureaucrat than a commercial party.

I was unable to attend the beginning of a particularly critical negotiation because of a scheduling conflict on another project. When I arrived late to the negotiations, one of my colleagues was bogged down on a sensitive point with the Chinese side, led by SDIC representatives. I took a back seat and listened as my colleague persisted rather persuasively through a translator. About

45 minutes into a particular point, I could not sit back any longer. I spoke up in Chinese to the lead Chinese negotiator who was a senior cadre in the Chinese Communist Party. I waxed on in native enough Chinese, and it appeared that the Chinese side was convinced with my position. Of course, he could not concede without some degree of pushback. And, so, after I finished, he paused, collected his thoughts and then began to speak. The first words out of his mouth were, *Su Tongzhi* (苏同志), "Comrade Su (my Chinese surname)." This was not the expected Mr. Su, Mr. Silk or just *Su Qi* (苏骐), my Chinese name, but "*Comrade* Su," a title reserved for a member of the Chinese Communist Party. Not more than a second after the words left his mouth he stopped, and turned to his colleague with a look on his face that clearly broadcast "Did I just call him *Comrade*?!" The whole room broke out in nervous laughter. I'm sure the negotiator was hoping that his fellow cadres didn't report the mishap to his superiors.

Comrade Who?

It was in this spirit of relative camaraderie that we concluded a suite of project documents that were good for the stakeholders (the Central Government, Gansu Provincial Government, and the foreign investor), the contractors (all of whom were instrumentalities of the Provincial Government), and the rate payers of Gansu. The documents would yield returns for the stakeholders, reward the contractors for good performance, but also impose appropriate penalties for failure to perform to agreed standards. And finally, the agreement brought much-needed foreign capital into the province to provide much-needed power for its residents and commercial and industrial users at a reasonable price of power.

Shandong Zhonghua Power Project

I also acted as counsel to the lenders in two watershed project financings at the very end of the 1990s: the Shandong Zhonghua Power Project that closed in 1998 and the Chengdu Water Project. As mentioned in the Prologue, this was China's first large-scale BOT water project, which achieved financial close in 1999 as Asia was emerging from its Financial Crisis.[6] Both of these projects—Shandong and Chengdu—contributed to the setting of the market standard by equitably managing the tremendous construction risks and conflicts of interests presented, as well as laying the foundation for an appropriate allocation of risks among foreign and domestic lenders standing alongside one another in financing.

The Shandong Zhonghua Power Project was a milestone in many respects. With an installed generating capacity of 3,000 MW and a total project cost of US$2.2 billion, it was, at the time, the largest foreign-invested power project to achieve financial close in China and one of the largest private-invested power projects, in terms of installed capacity, ever to have been financed on a limited-recourse basis. It was also the first multiple power project (four major power plants) in one foreign-invested joint venture company to achieve financial close in China. Shandong was the first project financing in China where local currency

---

6 For more detailed treatment of these projects, see Mitchell A. Silk and Thomas E. Brown, "The Shandong PRC milestone," *Project Finance International*, March 24, 1999, Issue 168, pp. 52-54; Mitchell A. Silk and Simon Black, "Case Study – Chengdu No 6 Water Plant," *Project Finance International*, Feb. 23, 2000, Issue 187.

(RMB) lenders ranked equally with USD lenders. This represented a turning point in funding sources for executing project financings in China.

Shandong provided a precedent and market standard for a number of rather complex issues of first instance that guided cross-border project finance in China and catalyzed activity in the project finance market. The most challenging issues arose out of project circumstances that had never confronted foreign lenders in China. First, the project presented complex construction risks because the financing supported four different large, base-load power projects, one of which was in commercial operation, one near construction completion, and two prior to the commencement of construction. Second, the lenders had to address numerous project sponsor conflicts of interest since the sponsors had multiple roles as equity investors, construction contractors, offtakers, operators, and fuel suppliers. Third, the intercreditor arrangement was highly nuanced and complex due to the fact that for the first time Chinese RMB lenders were lending a sizeable portion of project finance to a large-scale project alongside two groups of offshore foreign currency lenders, with each group taking different project risks.

The project structuring and development and documentation and negotiation of its financing took up over five years (and thousands of lawyer billable hours!) to bring the financing to completion due to the complexity of the transaction, its structure, and the sheer number of participants. The closing alone stretched over three days and nights. All of the hard work bore fruit, and the project provided a very solid precedent for the market standards relating to local currency negotiations.

Chengdu BOT Water Project

The Chengdu BOT Water Project closed at a challenging time for foreign investment in China—many of its Asian neighbors were still emerging from the impact of the Asian Financial Crisis (see Chapter 2). The Chengdu project provided an important benchmark for a number of key points of equitable risk allocation for the China project finance market and picked up where Shandong Zhonghua left off in terms of treatment of construction cost overrun risks under the project documents, regulatory risks relating to pricing and foreign exchange, and intercreditor issues among foreign commercial and development lenders, as well as local lenders. Seth and I both worked on the project—he as a banker advising one of the losing bidders and I as legal counsel to another of the losing bidders. At the close of bidding, I was eventually chosen as lenders' counsel for the winning bidder, and so worked on the project through financing closing. Sorry, Seth.

The Chengdu Water BOT Project was everything that the Shandong Zhonghua Power Project was not in terms of size and complexity. It was a relatively small municipal water project with a project cost of roughly US$106 million. The project had excellent sponsors—Vivendi, a large French industrial, and Marubeni, one of Japan's largest trading companies, who were supported by leading foreign commercial banks led by Crédit Lyonnais and, more important, the Asian Development Bank and the European Investment Bank. Notwithstanding its size, Chengdu presented its share of financing challenges and risks. The legal territory was relatively uncharted as it was the first water treatment project under China's emerging BOT regime. This was the first major project financing in China where the sponsors and their financiers were taking municipal (and not Central government) risk.

A 25+ Year Friendship

My interaction with Seth was limited to attending sessions that the Chengdu Municipal Authorities organized for the bidders to answer questions and provide clarifications on the bidding documents. We were indeed representing competing bidders, but Seth's questions and approach impressed me as highly professional and well-grounded in the basics of project finance theory. Thus, competition aside, Seth's professionalism and project finance expertise spoke to me then and when we crossed paths over 20 years later. At that dinner decades later, we marveled at how much we think alike on not just the *need*, but also the *how* of bringing the private sector into infrastructure in a bigger way. We chatted about all the memories in the last 30 years from our impressions of China to some giants we met along the way and also the travel tidbits like ordering food in native, even Cantonese.

The degree of municipal risk presented in this project was significant since the Chengdu Municipal Government guaranteed all performance and financial obligations of the local offtaker, with no recourse for the provincial or Central authorities. Extensive financial due diligence of the Chengdu counterparties assisted in understanding the contours of these risks. It helped that the project had the strong support of the Chinese Government, as well as two key multilateral development banks.

The Chengdu BOT Project presented the risks of tariff levels and adjustments, project approval risks, and foreign exchange risks (especially since project revenues were RMB-denominated and equity and debt was USD-denominated) that confronted other projects. The refined BOT process and documentation went a long way in addressing these issues. Specifically, the bidding documents that were ultimately used as the basis for the project contracts that the sponsors entered into with its Chengdu counterparties provided a clear basis for escalating the tariff over the term of the project in a clear and objective manner.

By the year 2000, these projects forged a clear set of market standards had emerged that guided foreign project financings. This market standard allowed emerging countries to tailor their policies to make a very hospitable environment for foreign infrastructure financing. This new clarity about how to engage with many emerging markets led to a veritable gold rush of foreign banks, lenders, and developers eager to take part in their growth. In this next chapter, we'll learn about what the gold rush was like on the inside for bankers like Seth, and how all this foreign activity affected the local markets.

CHAPTER 4

THE GIANTS RUSH EAST

By Seth Tan

After the Asian Financial Crisis crippled many emerging markets, the giants generally came from developed markets, particularly in the power sector. Some examples were AES and InterGen from the U.S., and EDF and Tractebel from Europe. These were large developers turned long-term investors, and they brought their technology, contractual structures, and financing tools to Southeast Asia. Their supply of capital, quality equipment, and advanced technology came with a price tag. While this price tag usually translated to marginally higher tariffs with consumers footing the bill, politicians were happy to swallow this pill in exchange for fewer complaints about lack of power and infrastructure.

Many Asian countries badly needed more electricity to support their industries and population, hence readily accepted these foreign giants with open arms. To attract long-term foreign investment into mega power projects, some projects offered very conducive conditions some referred to as bringing "Western conditions to Asian settings." These conditions cut across all project development phases and included adopting certain technical standards, authorizing equipment import tax exemptions, and waiving the immunity rights of relevant national government stakeholders. In one case where the local collateral security laws were not yet fully developed to give comfort to international lenders, a national act (law) was introduced to allow enforcement of project security and create amenable conditions for the specific project.

In the 1990s, a majority of all new privately owned electricity generating capacity financed in the developing world was in: **ASIA.**

In the case of the Philippines,

over **90**%

of new capacity installed during the 1990s came from foreign owned IPPs.

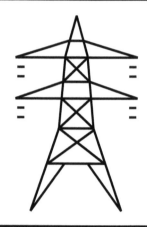

Although the initial investors were from USA and Europe, the growth of the sector also started to build up regional or even in-country champions.

Source: Woodhouse, E. J., "The IPP Experience in the Philippines," working paper, 2005, p. 16.

To be fair to some of these Southeast Asian governments, there were also instances in other regions like the Middle East where similar accommodations resulted in the successful attraction of international developers to invest in large-scale infrastructure projects. The public-private partnership (PPP) models had also resulted in large-scale developments of infrastructure in the West, hence it seemed a good idea to adopt these conditions to accelerate country developments in Asia.

A Lot of Cooks in the Kitchen

In the early aughts, large-scale power projects were considered country critical, hence national electricity utilities were prepared to enter into long-term power purchase agreements that were supported by central governments, often through a guarantee by the country's Ministry of Finance. This model enabled developed economies' export credit agencies (ECAs) to provide attractive political and commercial risk insurance, often north of 90% coverage and over 15 years long. This, in turn, allowed commercial banks to provide huge sums of financing on limited recourse basis.

This provided two critical benefits.

First, limited recourse was and continues to be a very important concept for the success of projects of this magnitude. Given the large power development needs in various Asian countries, the limited recourse models allowed commercial banks to fund majority of the project cost (often 70-75% for power projects), whilst not requiring developers to put up contingent support to cover the debt for all future risks. The high debt load for each project reduced the overall return requirements as debt is cheaper than equity. Limited recourse also allowed developers to fund more projects. Even for very large developers, it would be difficult to fund many projects if banks required them to put up a lot of equity or huge contingent support for each project.

Second, ECA support mitigates some of the tougher market and political risks presented.

An important needle mover was thus ECA coverage for political and commercial risks, and a big part of project preparation became about understanding the eligibility and processing requirements of ECAs.

Depending on where the project equipment was sourced and the country where the construction contractors came from, a single project could have multiple ECAs involved, resulting in various debt tranches. In the aftermath of the Asian crisis, banks were also more conservative in their individual ticket sizes, hence there were large bank clubs for each transaction as banks wanted to diversify their exposure.

The result we often saw was over 10 bankers from various banks sitting in the "war room" negotiating various aspects of the transaction with the developer. Some discussions were substantive, but others could be more technical (dull), like compliance with ECA requirements. Once or twice, I even saw some bankers dozing off during negotiations of the more technical meetings.

In contrast to the sea of bankers, the developers' team that sat across the negotiating table tended to be relatively small. They were, however, usually very experienced. In a sponsor-friendly era where there were perhaps too many banks eager to support quality sponsors and quality projects, the stage was set for some very gruesome negotiations on the project's financing. Dozing off at the table might mean you end up signing a deal your employer might not be very excited about!

The Scales Tipped

Whereas with most negotiations in any industry the lender or financier holds most of the cards, in this era, there were more bankers than developers! It was a gold rush! The most memorable example of this was Mr. M, who led a European developer negotiating team for a large gas-fired power project in Thailand. He was very smart but very impatient—a lethal combination. Even though it's years later, whenever I bump into fellow bankers who worked on the same project, we inevitably reminisce about Mr. M.

Mr. M was an extremely quick thinker. He could think through complex alternative scenarios very quickly and then would look triumphantly across the negotiating table. That really spooked some of the bankers. Hence, in some sessions, the bankers had their more junior representatives at the table, which further worked in Mr. M's favor. He was a master of process management and used these negotiation sessions to "lock in" certain agreements.

Mr. M was also quite ready to show his impatience and even anger. Years later, one banker recounted to me how Mr. M threw a water glass against the wall when progress on a particular matter moved too slowly for him. I also sat in one session where Mr. M scolded the bankers across the table for what felt like 30 minutes. The lead negotiator on the bank side of the table was an American banker who had operated in the region for many years. I watched as he sat silently while Mr. M unleashed his anger.

In the end, the deal reached successful financial close, and Mr. M got most of what he wanted through his management and negotiation style. However, some banks were not keen to work with Mr. M on subsequent projects. Nonetheless, his success showed how the scales had tipped because where developers had been the eager ones at the beginning of the foreign investment craze, the bankers became the eager ones.

A Lot of Kitchens!

In the ensuing years, the scales tipped once again as two phenomena emerged.

Firstly, it became apparent that adapting to local conditions in Asia increased in importance. Unlike foreign giants who are typically just governed by economic considerations, local decision-makers (particularly government officials) also had to consider non-economic issues. For example, I once had to visit offices on three different floors in a government agency to explain the same idea again and again. While the officials did not explain to me why I needed to do that, I could see the relief in the eyes of those I met later when I explained to them that the other offices were also supportive of the idea. Every project had not only a lot of cooks in the kitchen, but a lot of kitchens!

The second phenomenon is the emergence of regional giants, particularly from China. As we will see in the next chapter, Chinese banks, equipment suppliers, and sponsors began to emerge as dominant players in projects in their own home market.

CHAPTER 5

DEVELOPING MARKETS STANDING ON THEIR OWN TWO FEET

By Mitchell A. Silk

I n the very early 2000s, everyone working in project finance in China was wondering whether or not Chinese banks would take over the project finance market in China. This was due to the confluence of a number of critical market factors, namely developments in China's machine building and banking sectors. China's machine building sector was able to prove the technical standards and operational reliability of its domestic-produced power generating equipment, reducing the need for the import of relatively higher priced imported foreign equipment. At the same time, the domestic Chinese banking market was growing in size, liquidity, depth, and tenor. These two trends led to an interesting shift in the project finance market, with local People's Republic of China (PRC) banks emerging as key players displacing many foreign financiers. This, in turn, forced foreign developers and financiers to engineer more sophisticated and tailored financing products for an elite clientele willing to pay their premiums.

A Competitive Advantage

Up until the mid-1990s, foreign banks dominated project finance in the PRC. In 1995-96, a significant shift took place that began to tilt the hand toward PRC banks in project finance transactions. The changes were played out initially in the power sector where local manufacturers could now produce high-quality machinery acceptable to the international insurance and banking markets. The primary battle was fought between the ministries of power and machine building over the permissibility of imported power generating equipment. The power authorities pushed for technological advancement through imported equipment even if this meant higher project costs and therefore higher power prices. Machine building, on the other hand, was all for bolstering local industry. Machine building ultimately won out and a new regulation was put in place which mandated domestic generating equipment over imported equipment for units with generating capacities of up to 300 MW. The resulting comparative advantage of domestic equipment suppliers and contractors created a new demand for local currency borrowing with all of its attending challenges and risks.

From this point onward, PRC banks began to appear on the scene. The first notable appearance was on the Shandong Zhonghua Power Project. The Shandong Zhonghua Project originally planned to utilize U.S. generating equipment from Westinghouse, which had secured export credit support from the U.S. Export-Import Bank (U.S. EXIM). The Chinese partners in the project, however, had been frequently expressing concern over the cost of U.S. equipment and the financing requirements of foreign lenders like U.S. EXIM. As domestic Chinese generating equipment became acceptable to foreign lenders and insurers as proven technology and the depth of the long-term domestic PRC credit markets increased, the project's Chinese partners pushed for replacing U.S. equipment and lenders with domestic counterparts;[7] and that is exactly what happened. The transition was slow, and the sponsor negotiations were challenging, but it eventually became the first large project financing in China with a major PRC bank tranche.

The trend followed suit in other industries and local PRC banks began to emerge as dominant forces in various other credits. These transactions were not all project financed per se, but they were nonetheless structured. One example is the US$1.8 billion

---

7   Modern Power Systems. (1998, August 20). Chinese boiler contracts: Persistence pays off. www.modernpowersystems.com. Retrieved November 30, 2021, from https://www.modernpowersystems.com/features/featurechinese-boiler-contracts-persistence-pays-off/.

BP Sinopec Shanghai Ethylene financing—a landmark financing completed in January 2002—in which the foreign banks had a relatively small US$200 million of total commitments. I represented the lead arrangers on that financing, and it was truly a different dynamic than when foreign and Chinese banks stood alongside each other in the Shandong Zhonghua Power Project financing.

These financings shared the common traits of high capital intensity and funding domination by the PRC banks (even in respect to USD commitments). A uniform structure as to intercreditor matters (namely in respect to administration, defaults, and security sharing) began to emerge as between the foreign and local PRC banks.

Three Trends Which Elevated Chinese Banks

Three trends were behind the emergence of Chinese banks as dominant lenders in long-term industrial credits in China. First, the PRC regulators and banks had been struggling with managing the balance sheet impact of massive bad loan portfolios of the PRC banks. The position largely arose out of the PRC government's ambitious commercial bank and State-owned enterprise reform programs. Total nonperforming loans (NPLs) in the PRC banking system were at the time estimated at somewhere between US$217 billion[8] and US$630 billion.[9] To highlight the enormity of this issue, the total amount of these NPLs by far dwarfed the GDP of Hong Kong at the time, which was around US$175 billion. Addressing China's NPL crisis was central to the PRC's harmonizing its position in the international banking arena and ensuring that its banks satisfied basic international risk-based capital adequacy requirements. The effect was that the balance sheets of PRC banks had much greater capacity to handle large project financing initiatives.

---

8   The face amount of loans transferred to the four asset management companies formed at that time.

9   According to the IMF.

Second, the PRC banks found themselves flush with both RMB and USD funding. Very stringent balance of payments controls during and immediately after the Asian Financial Crisis put the PRC among the top in the world in terms of foreign exchange reserves. At the time, the PRC boasted reserves of over US$230 billion. The major PRC commercial banks were primary beneficiaries of this new position since the dearth of domestic investment outlets translated to high RMB deposit growth for the PRC banks. The banks were very eager to deploy these frothy deposit reserves since their USD deposit liabilities began to exceed their comparable currency loan assets by as much as 40%. At the same time, RMB reserves were also at a record high. This put them in a position flush with liquidity and eager for large financings.

Finally, while the PRC banks were amassing their vast funding sources, the foreign banks were licking their wounds from the non-bank financial institution crises that erupted in the late 1990s with the restructurings and failures of numerous window companies and international trust and investment corporations—Guangdong Enterprises, Yue Xiu, GITIC, GZITIC, and Fujian ITIC to name a few. In the wake of these restructurings and associated losses, foreign bank credit committees were generally skeptical if not reluctant to take on large China exposure.

These trends cumulatively gave rise to an increasing reliance on domestic PRC banks to meet the funding needs of a number of major project financings in the market.

Peaceful Coexistence and Symbiosis

In the wake of the cumulative impact of the Asian Financial Crisis (see Chapter 2) and Asia Bird Flu, the Hong Kong project finance markets were depressed in the very early 2000s. There was, however, a glimmer of hope in some large industrial project financing that were proceeding—including the US$1.4 billion Shell and CNOOC Nanhai Petrochemical (SECCO) project, the BASF and Sinopec US$1.4 billion Nanjing Ethylene project, and the US$150 million Krupp Shanghai Steel Mill Phase 2 project financing. These financings represented a new trend in project financings in China where there was often an even split of onshore and offshore commitments.

Beyond these few, many projects were on ice. Most leading foreign bankers took a longer-term view. Many of them recognized that command of the market is not measured solely in terms of levels of participating commitments in a particular loan. This includes structuring, credit analysis (and particularly the analysis of complex project risk derived from a jigsaw of many complex contracts), modeling, documentation and negotiation, and agency roles. As capable and experienced as some project finance officers at the PRC banks were becoming, there still were not nearly enough of them to go around. And this is where the foreign banks filled the gap.

By the very early 2000s, the PRC project finance market reached a new level of development in which PRC banks and foreign banks needed to work together to fully exploit the market.

On the level of origination, both groups of banks had their strong institutional corporate client bases that demanded both foreign and local banks in most, if not all, major financings for projects with foreign investment.

These clients wanted access to bankers to whom they could relate and who could appreciate country and project risks against the backdrop of broader, and in some instances, global relationships. This therefore pointed to a clear role for both foreign and local banking groups in projects where relationship banking is key.

As to underwriting, structuring, and credit analysis, the foreign banks clearly had considerably more know-how and certainly far more resources to successfully complete these tasks. This is why they were typically chosen to serve in due diligence, project risk analysis, technical, structuring, insurance, and modeling roles. Of course, expert Chinese input was always required as to domestic financial issues and other matters of local practice. Syndication and internal bank credit approvals were clearly areas where both foreign and local bank expertise are integral to the process where the project credit involves borrowings in both RMB and USD, which is invariably the case for almost all projects. Similarly, the foreign banks also found themselves leading documentation and negotiations utilizing their considerable knowledge and expertise in project management and related areas. Still, there was considerable room for cross-fertilization in this area.

An excellent example of this peaceful coexistence and symbiosis was the award-winning SECCO financing mentioned above. I led the team of lawyers representing the lenders. To say it was a big deal is an understatement. In sheer numbers, the project cost of the underlying petrochemical project that was a joint venture between two industry giants, Shell and Sinopec, was over US$2.6 billion and the total financing was the equivalent of US$1.8 billion. In addition to being the first major international project financing completed in China after the Asian Financial Crisis, the SECCO project was also distinguished in being the first mega-petrochemical project to reach financial close in China as well as the largest long-term financing led jointly by domestic and foreign banks that closed on an uncovered basis. In other words, the financing was not supported by any third-party credit enhancement. This latter point was highly significant because of the sheer size of the project and the complexity of risk presented.

The very end of the 1990s and early 2000s was a distinct turning point for offshore project financiers in China, as well as for domestic PRC project financiers. There were clear niches in the project finance market for both foreign and PRC banks. Yet, over time, the PRC banks came to dominate the domestic PRC project finance markets, in part due to commercial reasons, and in part due to the growth and maturity of their financial institutions.

Market barriers to foreign institutions played more than a small role in how the space evolved. Given the totality of circumstances, foreign project finance players have generally succeeded in areas where they played to their strengths, including where financing required more structured financing solutions or where the sponsors or projects *required* funding sources outside of China. The PRC banks took their final step in solidifying their position as international project financiers when they led a major tranche (roughly US$900 million) of the US$2.615 billion debt facility established to finance the US$5 billion Tangguh LNG Project in Indonesia. This was the first time that the PRC banks participated in a major way in a large project financing *outside* of China and in an emerging market, with all of the attending risks, alongside major international commercial banks and two leading development finance institutions (Japan Bank for International Cooperation and Asian Development Bank). All said and done, by the early 2000s, domestic PRC banks had already begun to stand on their own two feet in the realm of project finance.

At the time, you could find similar trends emerging globally as countries developed their own tailored market standards and used them to fuel growth in their own markets through infrastructure financing. In the next chapter, we'll flip points-of-view from an emerging market to a developed market. Seth will analyze his time in Australia and explore how its creation of a hospitable environment politically and commercially allowed its infrastructure market to flourish domestically and abroad.

CHAPTER 6

WALTZING MATILDA

By Seth Tan

n 2003, there was a hiring freeze on the Australian project finance team of my bank. Internal transfer was the only way to fill a vacated senior role, thus begun my overseas stint for most of the next 15 years. Living in Sydney and covering the power and utilities market in all of Australia was a great move for me. On a personal level, having lived and worked only in Singapore prior to that, it was a pleasant surprise to learn more about work-life balance. As you can imagine, some experiences were quite the culture shock for me. Never before had I experienced going to a mate's barbecue and ending up meeting close to 100 people throughout the day as friends invited their friends who invited their friends and so on. There were similar pleasant surprises inside the office, for instance on some Friday late afternoons there would be "Beer O'clock" where colleagues just kick back, drink beer, and discuss "work" in more leisurely settings.

As far as project finance goes, it was also an eye-opener as I found it amazing that although the population was only around 20 million people, it was one of the largest infrastructure financing markets in Asia. So, I took advantage of my time there—four years—to understand what the levers and gears were that created this massive market.

There were three important characteristics to the Australian market that I think made it incredibly powerful in the infrastructure finance arena.

#1: Grandfathering

I noticed early on that the Australian government created a very enabling environment for this sort of investment. One phrase I heard from time to time in Aussie deals was "grandfathering," which allowed contracts or infrastructure projects to continue to operate under previously approved terms, even though the regulations have changed. This, I thought, was a good representation of a broader approach that the government consciously undertook to attract private sector investment in infrastructure. Grandfathering gave the strong signal of long-term stability for projects that were already approved, and this created more confidence amongst the private sector, especially for infrastructure where payback cannot be fully achieved in one political election cycle. Consequently, private sector investments and financing poured not just into greenfield (to-be-constructed) projects, but also into the sale of brownfield (already completed and operating) infrastructure by past international owners, and for privatization of state-owned infrastructure.

#2: Conducive Commercial Structures

Another important lever I thought was conducive commercial structures. For instance, given the importance assigned to utility assets by the government, project finance banks felt very confident in their dealings, so much so that they could view these assets as if they were dealing with large and established corporations. In practice, this means they extended shorter tenor loans with a large balloon repayment at loan maturity. That "mini-perm" structure became pervasive for regulated utility assets (like gas or power distribution) as banks believed (correctly) that the assets would continue to earn revenue beyond the current regulatory period (in many cases five years only). This structure is quite different from classical project finance, which required the loan to be fully repaid during the life of the initial project revenue contract (like a power purchase agreement). This often came with some contract life tail so there were some buffer years between the last loan repayment and the end of the project revenue contract, in case of an adverse event that required an extension of the loan repayment period.

Another conducive commercial structure was the fact that the tariff rate (and underlying cost) would reset every regulatory period. This allowed project owners to factor in new capital costs needed to keep the asset updated and the cost of associated equity and debt required to fund the existing and additional asset base. As the loan tenor was shorter (typically three and five years) than the classical project finance tenor of more than 10 years, loan pricing was also relatively lower.

However, for this commercial structure to work, it required rigorous to-and-fro interactions between the regulator and the project owners so that the proposed cost and revenue could be appropriately reviewed. If the government lacked the capacity to properly review the proposals submitted by the project owners, there was a risk it could lead to unnecessary capital expenditure and an increase in tariff.

#3: Proper Project Preparation

At every step, quality consultants were involved to ensure that government initiatives and projects were well prepared. This of course made the Aussie infrastructure market a professional services heaven, but the end result was better-prepared projects in general. As the project preparation approach was across the infrastructure sector, a common language emerged between the sponsors and their stakeholders (including the project finance banks). Combined with the gentlemanly business culture, deal origination was much faster than in many emerging economies.

Growing Into Giants

Against the conductive backdrop, private infrastructure involvement in Australia has been above 50% since 2003, but the port sector was even higher.

Overall, Australia was a place that made it "easy" to grow into a giant. In one of the earliest project finance cases I worked on, I had three key issues with the sponsors' proposal. I rolled up my sleeves and readied myself to argue like when I was in Asia across

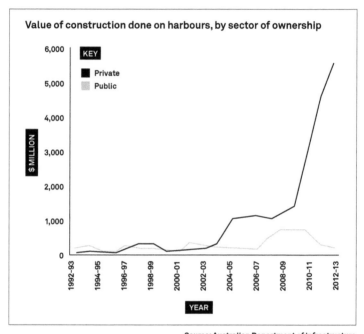

Source: Australian Department of Infrastructure and Regional Development, Information Sheet 52.

the table from Mr. M (see Chapter 4). To my surprise, the sponsors indicated they could accept items 1 and 2 but item 3 was an issue for them and wanted my deeper analysis on why I objected. After we figured it out, that transaction closed in less than six months.

The market conditions that evolved from these backdrops were consequently very conducive for growing local giants (sponsors). As previous waves of international sponsors left for various reasons, the stability and quality of the underlying infrastructure allowed even smaller players to step up, and debt financiers were able to provide a sizable portion of limited recourse financings even for acquisition assets. As part of a project finance consortium, I supported one such transaction in 2004 where Alinta (a Western Australia energy company) acquired a huge portfolio of regulated assets from U.S. company Duke Energy, which had to exit the market. The acquisition significantly increased the size of Alinta, and the company went on to make further acquisitions. In subsequent years, financier investors like Macquarie, Babcock & Brown, and many others were also successful in acquiring other infrastructure assets.

To be objective, it was not always hunky-dory as there were infrastructure cases that failed. There were sponsors of regulated utilities who pushed the reset tariffs too high, which affected affordability. There were acquisitions where too much was paid in order to win, but subsequent operations and maintenance was minimized and that affected the performance of infrastructure over time. And there were consultants who made too rosy predictions, which did not turn out to be true. Nonetheless, the Aussie market was very vibrant because its underlying conditions were generally conducive to closing quality transactions.

The years I was there also coincided with a resource boom because there was huge demand from China for mining resources like iron ore to support development and urbanization. This in turn accelerated the need for more infrastructure—including power and gas infrastructure—in Australia.

At this point in infrastructure finance history, we might call it the Renaissance—everyone and their friends were making masterpieces and almost every market had some sort of foreign collaboration going on for an infrastructure project. It seemed like giants were sprouting up in every market and at every possible angle. In the next chapter, Mitch will explore what happens when these giants and their projects started to get a bit too confident and a bit too big for their breeches.

CHAPTER 7

WHEN IT LOOKS TOO GOOD TO BE TRUE, IT IS

By Mitchell A. Silk

As a global market standard for project documentation and finance and security agreements began to emerge, the dance floor got a bit crowded with giants. When Chinese lenders began to grow in the foreign-investment market in China, clear stress lines started to appear at the project level. The performance of many foreign-invested projects with solid structures and rational financing arrangements ranged from satisfactory to well. But others, particularly those that tested the market standards and were perhaps a bit too rich, were confronted with financial, legal, commercial, and technical challenges.

Pounding the Pavement

From 1992 to 1996, my work as an associate at Chadbourne & Parke provided me with foundational knowledge of Chinese project finance. The schooling I received served me well throughout my career. As an associate, I learned a lot from the partners I worked for as well as opposing counsel. However, my best education came from my clients. I was constantly on the road with power developer clients in China, learning the technical and financial dimensions of the energy business. The challenges were mainly in the backwaters of China—as I mentioned earlier, Gansu Province in China's northwest at the edge of the Gobi Desert, as well as Yingkou, Yantai, and Harbin in China's northeast Heilongjiang Shandong and Liaoning Provinces; Wuhan and Zhengzhou in Central China; and Guangzhou, Shenzhen, and Xiamen in Southeastern China.

These clients provided me with a priceless education in the power and infrastructure business from some of the world's leading power and infrastructure developers, engineers, and financial analysts. I forged an especially close relationship with James "Jim" Wood, then a senior executive at Babcock & Wilcox. Jim, who started his career at B&W as a boiler engineer and slowly worked his way up, taught me the ropes of power development and finance. Jim taught me all about the technical aspects of steam generation and power production, transmission, and distribution, and his financial analysts schooled me in the design and financial engineering of financial models for power projects. This detailed knowledge greatly enhanced my ability to draft and negotiate long and technical agreements for power project financing. Jim later went on to become the CEO of B&W and a senior official in the U.S. Department of Energy

Rigdon Boykin was the Chadbourne partner who brought me to Hong Kong, and he was an exceptional mentor during this period. Rigdon was, in personality and appearance, different from the representative Hughes Hubbard partner that I was used to. He was short, stout, and spoke with the Southern drawl of his native South Carolina. At the negotiating table and internal strategy sessions, he was, however, larger than life and an exceptional lawyer. He profoundly shaped the legal terrain supporting the birth and growth of independent power development in the United States through the litigation that he led up to the U.S. Supreme Court on behalf of the American Paper Institute in the early 1980s.[10] These cases were a linchpin in the growth and development of applying project finance techniques to capital intensive private power projects in the United States.

Rigdon had a novel and refreshingly entrepreneurial approach to the practice of law. He didn't wait for work to come in the door. He went out and got it. He would travel throughout China, identify power generation projects ripe for foreign investment, secure

---

10 See *Federal Energy Regulatory Commission v. Mississippi*, 456 US 742 (1982), and *American Paper Institute, Inc. v. American Electric Power Service Corporation*, 461 US 402 (1982). Rigdon represented the American Paper Institute in both cases; in the former as an *amicus* party, and in the latter as the lead appellant.

rights in those projects, and then bring clients into his projects. In exchange, he would require the clients to retain his law firm for the legal work and also to grant the firm a carried interests in the profits of the venture. In addition to the education in the practice of energy and project finance law I received from Rigdon, I gained invaluable skills at the negotiation table. I also learned some exceptional and entertaining phrases—some not so kosher, like "Pigs get fat and hogs go to the market!" In more kosher and industry-specific terms, "a deal that is too rich for one side is doomed for everyone." Or, as the "grandfather" of the law and practice of infrastructure finance, Graham Vinter says, "It's all about equitable risk allocation, and ensuring that the party in the best position to control the risk should own the risk."

During the next phase of foreign-investment in the Chinese power sector, there were more than a few projects that skated too close to the edge of this basic rule. We'll discuss a big one next: the Meizhou Wan Power Project.

Pigs get fat, hogs go to market.

Meizhou Wan or Bust

Meizhou Wan was a 724 MW coal-fired power plant—the first foreign-invested power plant in the southeast province of Fujian, and the first wholly foreign owned power project in the whole of China. The sponsor group was exceptionally strong: leading international power developers InterGen, Lippo China Resources (a subsidiary of one of Indonesia's strongest conglomerates with strong China ties and whose founder hailed from Fujian Province), and El Paso Corp. In addition, a particularly strong lending group supported the project. The commercial bank syndicate included BNP Paribas (then Banque Paribas), BA Asia, UFJ Bank (then Tokai Bank), and CSFB. In addition, the Asian Development Bank provided a direct loan and co-financing facility, and the Spanish (CESCE) and French (COFACE) also provided export credit facilities. The fact that the project achieved financial closing amid the Asian Financial Crisis led many to believe in the great strengths of the project. In retrospect, it shouldn't have been hard to imagine what might happen to a hog that had grown this fat and happy.

The market, commercial, and political circumstances were not kind to the project. As a general matter, the Asian Financial Crisis and other domestic Chinese macroeconomic and credit market factors imposed more than the normal financial pressures on foreign-invested projects. Significant reforms were afoot by the early 2000s. These reforms were driven by both evolving government-wide economic policies as well as in the power-sector-specific reforms relating to foreign direct investment in China. Rapid growth in the power sector also brought challenges relating to rational grid management and supply and demand within the system. The Central Government also began to rethink State ownership in the sector, prompting the restructuring of State-owned interests in the power sector. These factors and other prompted local competition and national interest. There were also constant reviews and reforms in foreign direct investment policy. This is all to say, it was a time of massive upheaval and this was the general policy backdrop against which the Meizhou Wan project played out.

Many of the project's very strengths were the root cause of its financial issues. Its strong foreign sponsor group required a high equity return. The engineering, procurement, and construction (EPC) contract was more expensive than similar contracts because of the risk premiums and the fact that the project utilized foreign equipment. In addition to equity costs being relatively high, the strong protections of all tranches of the project debt also came with a relatively higher debt price tag. Further, the offtake agreement included newfangled protections such as 100% of foreign costs being fully indexed. And, finally, the project had a long-term coal supply contract for imported Indonesian coal.

It didn't matter—everything came out in the wash. The marginally higher equity and debt, coal supply, EPC and foreign exchange fluctuation protection costs all drove up the price of Meizhou Wan power to a level higher than comparable coal-fired plants in Fujian Province. Fingers started to point in all directions. Payments were withheld. Operational permits were delayed. In no time, the project was in a full-blown restructuring that continued over a period of several years.

In disputes and restructurings, there is never one party that is completely in the right or completely in the wrong, and there are never complete winners or complete losers. However, the Meizhou Wan project did not end as well for the foreign sponsors as other foreign-invested power projects in China. Domestic PRC lenders eventually took out the foreign lenders and replaced the US$566 million of foreign currency-denominated loans for local currency loans.

As some experts and journalists pointed out,[11] the project was burdened with disproportionately high costs of foreign participation—an expensive construction contract executed by one partner (Bechtel) comprising roughly 70% of the project cost, relatively higher coal costs for fuel supplied by another partner (an affiliate of the Lippo Group), and relatively higher equity returns for foreign currency-denominated equity (for all of the shareholders in the wholly foreign-owned project company) and the foreign debt. All of these marginally higher costs were passed through in the pricing for the power that the plant generated that

---

11 "Power cutting," IJGlobal, published June 1, 2004, https://ijglobal.com/articles/
    115412/power-cutting.

the Fujian Provincial Electric Power Bureau (FPEPB) had to pay under the power purchase agreement (PPA), and ultimately passed through to the consumers. This much higher than average overall power cost rose to a level that the FPEPB simply was not prepared to pay. The economic and certainly political costs were just way too high.

The disagreements over the underlying cost structure led to dispute after dispute between the project company and the FPEPB, and eventually to numerous payment defaults under the PPA. Without its lifeline of payments under the PPA, the project company was crippled and unable to meet debt service, leading to defaults under the loan documents. The project company was at its knees, and this served financially as the key motivating factor driving the restructuring of the project, and for domestic lenders taking out the foreign lenders.

As one expert so aptly put it at the time:[12]

> "For Meizhou Wan, the problem wasn't just the tariff, but many other key elements. In fact, Meizhou Wan provides a great lesson in how not to go about power projects in China.... The project company is handicapped for being a wholly foreign owned venture and is unable to benefit from the local clout that a joint venture scheme can draw on through its Chinese partner. Its fuel supply and financing, at least until recently, were drawn entirely from foreign sources. It was built with a very high cost EPC contract. And because of the nature of the financing, fuel supply and EPC contract, it produces power at a cost far above that of other generators in the province."

The Meizhou Wan project underlines the importance of Rigdon's statement of fundamental deal economics—"pigs get fat and hogs go to the market." The basic rule is, if you stay within the guidelines—that

---

12 ibid.

is, under the radar through commercial reasonableness and equitable risk allocation—the deal is most likely to sustain itself happily. If, however, a deal pushes some boundaries and is too rich for one party and inflames rate payers with its higher cost structure, the deal will risk regulatory and commercial scrutiny and risk consequences.

Two other major foreign-invested power projects that revised their tariff structures and refinanced out part of their foreign debt with local debt, the Shandong Zhonghua Power Project and Laibin B Power Project, are cases in point. Both projects came under pressure to revise their power tariffs and ultimately restructured their debt, but both projects did so off of sound project documents based on market standards that reflected equitable risk allocation. Rigdon's basic rule has been a constant guiding factor for me throughout my career in project finance, especially when analyzing the components of fundamental revenue streams and cost structures, particularly costs that may be passed through to users of infrastructure commodities, and the political dimensions attending those costs.

If anyone on either side of the deal insists on burdening the project with disproportionately rich returns, they risk diminishing and even losing their investment.

Sometimes, the drive for disproportionately rich returns was the result of persistent and aggressive developers pushing the limits or an extremely lax or hospitable—perhaps too hospitable—regulatory environment. As we'll see in the next chapter, this became particularly clear in the rapid adoption of windfarm technology in emerging markets. Windfarm development is no less technically and financially complex and challenging than a large base-load coal-fired power plant, requiring the same sort of risk allocation and due diligence to achieve success. When certain countries such as India created too many financial incentives to drive windfarm developments, the result was a frenzy of transactions mainly helmed by people more excited to join the bandwagon and make some cash than to create sustainable, long-term energy projects.

CHAPTER 8

CHASING WINDMILLS

By Seth Tan

The best and worst part of infrastructure life is that you don't get to be home a lot. For me, home extended to the food that I grew up with (小时候的味道). There was a point when I started to miss chicken rice so much that I would purposely take my time at Singapore's Changi Airport in order to savor another dish. It dawned on me that my days in Australia were probably over. Fortunately, I caught up with the next trend in our business: infrastructure funds.

Between 2003-2007, Australia was one of the largest superannuation markets in the world, and given infrastructure often provide very long-term and relatively stable cash returns, it was not surprising that institutional investors who managed third-party monies from the likes of insurance and pensions started to invest in this asset class. With the success of these funds in Australia, some decided to expand into Asia, and so began my new phase of working for one of them—Babcock and Brown. I spent the next two years flying up and down China, India, and several Southeast Asian countries looking for renewables assets to invest in.

With most of the good hydropower resources in the region already tapped, wind power seemed like the next electricity sector segment that was going to scale up. In 2008, wind power required a lower electricity tariff than solar power to be economical, and for countries like China and India, the potential for wind power was huge based on general wind assessments. These were gigantic markets, and both China and India were keen to increase the amount of wind power in their total energy mix. As such, they both introduced very attractive policies to grow this sector. However, not everyone knew the intricacies of wind power yet, and it turns out the fundamentals were more complex than they seemed.

The result was that some of these little piggies went to market before they could even have the chance to turn into hogs.

Winding Up

The first trip I made to China was to a location called 包头 (direct English translation could be "Wrapped Head"). From there, I would visit many potential wind sites in Inner Mongolia. The higher wind energy sites (or Class 1 wind sites) in China were mostly in remote high-altitude locations like Inner Mongolia and the government tried to facilitate thousands of megawatts of wind power development by earmarking "wind bases."

On this first trip, I drove for more than half an hour and all I saw were wind power projects as far as the eye could see. However, not every one of them was generating power. As Inner Mongolia was relatively far away from the larger electricity demand centers like Shandong and Beijing, strong long-distance transmission lines were needed but not yet built. Many of the wind projects were actually completed but had no way of delivering power. Those that *were* connected to the local grid faced a level of curtailment (i.e., not 100% of the electricity generated could be taken by the grid) as the local transmission grid was not built to take on so much intermittent electricity. As wind was not consistently blowing through the day and would vary from season to season, there were only certain times wind power was generated. The huge wind bases meant that when wind power was generated, the local grid had to suddenly take on large amounts of electricity.

There were also individual project issues. At the time there were no hard requirements on who could develop wind power projects so some developers turned out to be very ill-equipped. One sponsor I met used to be a Chinese calligrapher with some family wealth. Another sponsor used to own a coal mine and thought—given that he could be a financial sponsor of a coal mine—he could also be one for a wind power project. The reality was that he could not.

Unlike coal mining, which had an established industry standard and a huge ecosystem of service providers, the wind industry was then too nascent and had neither. In the end, the projects of the Chinese calligrapher and the coal mine investor fared worse than the adjacent wind power projects. In an almost funny situation, the staff of the calligrapher tried to convince me that wind data taken from a weather station that was 25 km away from the proposed site could be used as the primary data for assessing the site. I had no choice but to refuse to consider this project as the assessment for the project would likely be inaccurate.

After I saw a few of these, I decided to focus on wind sites closer to the electricity demand centers and, more important, smaller sites, so curtailment was less of an issue. But visiting these faraway sites in Inner Mongolia was an eye opener as to the overall state of the industry at that time.

Do you know?

Compared to conventional power which can generate electricity over 90% of a year given stable fuel supply, renewables like wind only generate around one-third of a year. Hence there was initially the need for additional support to make renewables economic to investors. To pay for this support, some governments adopt "polluter pays" mechanisms. The biggest of such "carrots and sticks" mechanism was the Kyoto Protocol (an international treaty that operationalized the 1992 United Nations Framework Convention on Climate Change, or UNFCC). In the first commitment period of 2008-2012, 36 countries supported greenhouse gas emission reduction. Some of the countries could not fully meet the targets on their own and hence funded emission reductions in other countries. With additional financial support, many renewables projects became economic and were developed during this period. The large market presented in turn accelerated technology innovation. The second commitment period (named Doha Amendment) however did not commence. It did not get the minimum numbers of countries to support as there were reportedly disagreements on how much one country should support another.

Windia

The wind power industry in India was going through equally dramatic changes. At that time, the Indian government introduced an incentive that allowed 80% accelerated (upfront) tax depreciation of wind power investments. That enabling policy changed the entire industry.

Given the rich incentive, many wind turbine manufacturers decided to build and operate wind farms, even though it wasn't their core expertise. Some even went to the extent of dividing the wind farms into investment packages of two to three wind turbines each so rich individuals could also invest in these wind farms akin to the many wealth investment products. When I visited a site in Rajasthan near the Blue City, I was offered the choice of investing in a few wind turbines next to the three wind turbines where a famous Bollywood star had indicated interest to invest in.

As the returns to the investment were mostly upfront, there was little reason for investors to scrutinize how well the wind farms were built. Were the wind measurements correctly taken? Were the wind and energy resource studies correctly performed? Were the wind farms' layout maximizing the energy generation? Were they able to generate the level of electricity as planned? Were there climatic issues like icing that could affect the wind farm's performance in some seasons? Was there potential risk of curtailment? These were some of the questions I had become used to asking in projects in Australia and Northeast Asia but the developers of the wind farms I was investigating either did not have the level of detail I required or were not personally equipped to answer me. The quality of the wind turbine equipment was itself sometimes called into question as some projects were clearly not performing at the level they advertised.

Today, investors and financiers often complain about the lack of proper incentives and enabling policies to attract them to support infrastructure. It is true in many cases. However, the wind power evolution in countries like China and India showed that partial-enabling or over-enabling can also cause problems. In the case of the 80% accelerated tax depreciation, as it was the first time the country was scaling up a new type of infrastructure like wind farms, checks and balances were not fully put into place, and the consequence was it increased the risk of moral hazard in the industry, and policies with good intentions inadvertently resulted in poor behavior by market players.

Whilst project level checks and balances are important, the right checks and balances could also be a very important pillar to successfully scale up a new type of infrastructure in a country or a series of projects in emerging countries.

Nonetheless, these trials and tribulations were all to be expected on an emerging market's journey; they were learning how to dance as giants.

As we can see by now, whether it's in regards to the financing or the technical knowhow, infrastructure markets have a predictable cycle: First they invite foreign investment for the newer technologies or funding sources not available on the ground, then they experience growth and development in their infrastructure, then they learn the tricks of the trade and their local suppliers, investors and bankers are strengthened, and then projects become increasingly domestic run and domestic funded. As we'll see in the next chapter, the final step of this cycle for many countries, including China, is that once they have the infrastructure they need and their local financing markets are deep and stable, they begin to seek opportunities outside their borders. That is, they become the foreign investors (giants) in other emerging markets.

CHAPTER 9

FROM CASH-STRAPPED TO FLUSH WITH CASH

By Mitchell A. Silk

At the turn of the millennium, there was a fundamental shift of capital flows in China's energy and infrastructure sector. Namely, Chinese money started flowing outward rather than foreign money flowing inward. Around the same time, I started to plan a transition back to the United States. I was a junior partner and saw an opportunity to ride the outbound investment wave and assist in building out Allen & Overy's New York office, which was in growth mode. I was engaged on three outbound mandates in Latin America, two in Brazil and one in Colombia, and those projects provided an excellent base for me to straddle my transition back to New York, with the convenience of being closer to the deals.

China Goes Outbound

For reasons discussed in Chapter 5, foreign developers, equipment providers, and financiers were finding themselves in more limited roles on Chinese projects. When they did find roles, they had to seize specific opportunities where they were able to provide unique, value-add solutions.

This domestic market shift, combined with other domestic market dynamics, led to an even more interesting trend in the project finance space: Chinese investors and their financiers were expanding abroad through outbound direct investment (ODI) in the foreign energy and infrastructure sector.

China first started to dip its toe in ODI waters in 1979. Until 1985, these initiatives were dominated by mainly Central Government policy-driven acquisition needs and conducted exclusively by State-owned Enterprises. The activity was relatively modest, with only 189 ODI projects approved during that period, totaling just under US$200 million in investments. Liberalizations in China led to greater activity in ODI during the period from 1986 to 1991. The Chinese Government expanded the list of destination countries for Chinese ODI and also allowed private enterprises to invest abroad. ODI activity picked up during this period with a total of 891 approved projects representing US$1.2 billion in investment activity. China continued to open, and further liberalization led to ODI doubling in dollar amount to US$2.4 billion from 1992 to 1998.

China's big push commenced in 1999 with the announcement of its "Going Global" strategy, which was designed to promote the international competitiveness of Chinese corporations. Energy, infrastructure, and natural resources featured prominently in the program. The new strategy led to a surge in ODI activity in the energy and infrastructure areas, both in terms of Chinese direct equity investments and Chinese debt financing and credit support—much of which benefitted from new Chinese Government subsidies, export credits, development loans, and other preferences like export tax rebates. ODI numbers soared, particularly in energy and infrastructure.

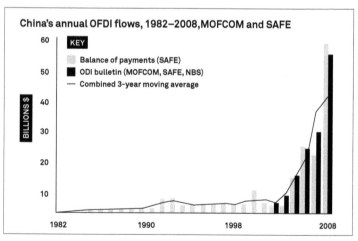

Source: https://www.piie.com/system/files/documents/pb09-14.pdf

China entered into an intensified phase of infrastructure ODI when it announced its One Belt, One Road (OBOR) program in

2013. OBOR is a massive global infrastructure ODI program, which was codified in the PRC Constitution in 2017 and grew into the present Belt and Road Initiative (BRI). China has conducted the vast majority of its recent ODI activity in infrastructure under BRI.

There was an interesting parallel between how foreign investors and developers could expect to be treated in China and how Chinese investors and developers could expect to be treated when working in other countries. Namely, China found itself constantly confronted with the same political risk issues that it pushed back so hard on when foreign investors came to China. Many of the issues referred to in previous discussions of the Market Standard for project finance in China revolve around political risk, including the consequences of acts of political force majeure, a change of law or policy, a breach of contract by a government counterparty, or foreign exchange convertibility or remittability. Interestingly, in its ODI activity abroad, the Chinese State-owned enterprises (and private companies as well) found themselves advocating for the very positions in their investments abroad as foreigners tried for projects in China. The roles have reversed, with emerging countries similarly looking to "push back" on risk overprotections. Nonetheless, the global experience China was gaining in infrastructure strengthened the Market Standards for everyone.

China's Financing Challenges and Political Resistance in the Fertile American Renewables Market

China did not achieve the desired results in all energy and infrastructure markets and sectors. The U.S. renewables market, for instance, was one pocket where China didn't fare that well.[13] The U.S. represented a massive market with tons of opportunities,

---

13 For a fuller discussion, see Gary Lazarus and Rebecca Perkins, "The Changing Landscape of the U.S. Energy Market: Is China Taking Over the World? The Case of China's Entry Into the U.S. Wind Power Sector," *Allen & Overy Thought Leadership Series* (Summer 2011 booklet); and Gary Lazarus, Noah Baer, and Lillian Samet, "The Political Dimensions of China's Entry Into the U.S. Solar Power Sector," *Allen & Overy Thought Leadership Series* (Summer 2011 booklet).

especially given the Chinese edge on wind turbine and solar panel supply and export credit support.

The growth potential was astounding and you would think it would have been a shoo-in. In the 2000s, China had witnessed astronomic domestic growth in wind and solar power generation, manufacturing, and overall industry capability. Growth of China's installed wind power capacity during the early 2000s is a case in point: the country realized low double-digit growth in 2003 and 2004, saw an astounding 64% growth in 2005, and achieved growth spurts in excess of 100% growth per annum through the end of the decade. In the Chinese domestic market, these advancements led to fierce competition, driving Chinese suppliers, developers, and their financiers to seek, pardon the pun, greener pastures abroad.

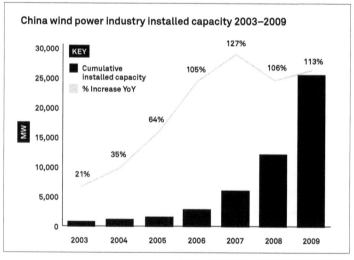

China wind power industry installed capacity 2003–2009

Source: BTM Consult, International Wind Energy Development: World Market Update, 2010.

At the time, both Europe and the U.S. presented the largest overseas renewables markets. Due to technological advancements and an improved regulatory environment, U.S. solar installation began hyper growth in 2008, and growth in the sector actually doubled in 2011-12 in terms of installed capacity and nearly doubled in monetary terms in 2010 when the market grew from US$3.6 billion to US$6 billion. A key factor behind this growth was the Renewable Portfolio Standards ("RPS") implemented by 29 states and the District of Columbia.

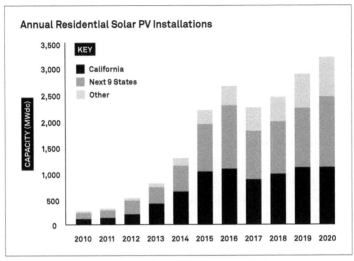

Source: SEIA/Wood Mackenzie Power & Renewables U.S.
Solar Market Insight 2020 Year In Review.

Chinese turbine manufacturers first tried Europe, especially Germany, Spain, and Italy, which all offered large market potential, incentives, and subsidies supportive of renewable energy projects. Chinese wind interests made limited success penetrating the European market and then the Global Financial Crisis hit and limited their prospects even more. Governments around the world were tightening their belts. By 2008, countries like Spain and Italy significantly cut their financial support for renewables by freezing or lowering tariffs, the revenue lifeline for investors. This was the death knell for many European renewables projects, not just those involving Chinese investment.

This contraction in Europe shifted Chinese renewables investors' focus to the United States. It seemed like a match made in heaven—put eager developers with low-cost equipment into a high-demand environment and one would have thought that this would yield a ton of deal activity. To the contrary, Chinese equipment suppliers had achieved astounding domestic renewables growth, but yet Chinese turbine suppliers had not even scratched the surface of the U.S. market by 2010. The result was baffling because Chinese turbines at the time were 20% less expensive than U.S. or European turbines. So what happened?

Financing and warranties were key roadblocks that Chinese investors, manufacturers, and developers ran into. While they scored big wins at home when international banks and insurers deemed Chinese coal-fired power-generating equipment proven technology, getting U.S. lenders and insurers to view Chinese wind turbine technology as proven technology was an unexpected challenge.

This left Chinese equipment suppliers and sponsors of U.S. projects willing to use Chinese technology with only limited options, most of which translated to increased financing costs. The options included borrowing offshore from Chinese or other relationship banks, financially backstopping warranties backing the Chinese equipment, or sponsors taking direct balance sheet risk through equity financing. Each of these options presented additional risk and/or marginal capital costs. Borrowing from Chinese or other non-U.S. relationship banks required getting those banks comfortable with all aspects of lending in the U.S. to a U.S. borrower with all the related regulatory and legal risks. Warranty backstops to Chinese turbine manufacturers required U.S. lenders to get comfortable with domestic Chinese counterparty risk or for the turbine manufacturers to arrange financial instruments to backstop these risks at a cost that would eat into equity margins. Finally, equity financing was simply an issue of prohibitively high capital costs in a low-margin development market.

The Labor Unions Step In

On top of these financial challenges, Chinese wind developers and equipment vendors also met stiff political opposition in their pursuit of market share in the U.S. The political winds started to blow heavy in late 2009 in response to an application to the

U.S. Department of Energy (DOE) for subsidized loan support for a private-invested wind project in Texas utilizing Chinese equipment. The Hill and various labor unions did not react well to a DOE-funded project that was seemingly taking away American jobs. In 2010, the United Steelworkers union (USW) filed a formal 301 complaint—which was 5,800 pages in its full glory—with the U.S. Trade Representative (USTR) claiming that the project was relying on unfair Chinese subsidies. China's Ministry of Commerce responded in kind, but with a mere 300-pages response.

As proceedings, including formal U.S.-China trade talks on the issue, were playing out before the USTR, then Chinese Premier Hu Jintao visited the U.S. in January 2011. The wind energy issue was one of many bilateral trade and investment issues that Premier Hu raised. In fact, several U.S. and Chinese companies produced letters of intent on a variety of energy investments, but the fact remains that Chinese wind interests never really entered the U.S. market in any meaningful way.

A Steely Response

This is an example of the political dimension of project development in energy and infrastructure. The projects are, by nature, typically large and capital intensive with considerable labor and other economic impacts. They therefore tend to be subject to considerable political scrutiny. Matters have not changed much over the last decade in the wind energy space. There has been minimal China investment in the wind space since Premier Hu's visit in 2011, and billionaire Sun Guangxin's recent attempt to develop a utility-scale wind farm with Chinese investment has been marred in politics.[14]

Chinese solar panel manufacturers have made considerably better inroads into the U.S. market; however, Chinese solar project developers fared only a little bit better than their wind energy counterparts. Chinese panel manufacturers have always had a toehold on the U.S. market, and Chinese solar companies have realized limited success in opportunistic purchases of U.S. solar technology companies out of bankruptcy (such as Hanergy's acquisition of MiaSole, Shunfeng's acquisition of Suniva, and GCL's acquisition of certain polysilicon assets of SunEdison). However, Chinese solar power developers have not realized notable traction in developing, owning, and operating U.S. solar power facilities.

Latin America Beckons

While China's European and U.S. endeavors didn't pan out as expected, it did experience measured growth in its other ODI efforts, including in Africa, Latin America, and the Middle East. I worked on multiple ODI projects involving two of China's state-owned energy and infrastructure enterprises: Sinopec and China Harbour Engineering Corp. (CHEC). Sinopec commenced an intense effort in the early 2000s to expand upstream oil and

---

14   Hyatt, J. (2021, August 9). *Why a Secretive Chinese Billionaire Bought 140,000 Acres of Land in Texas.* Forbes. Retrieved November 30, 2021, from https://www.forbes.com/sites/johnhyatt/2021/08/09/why-a-secretive-chinese-billionaire-bought-140000-acres-of-land-in-texas/

gas reserves through its subsidiary International Petroleum Exploration and Production Corporation (SIPC). At the same time, CHEC began an aggressive program to seek out opportunities in its core area of competence, large port and surface transportation projects.

I witnessed this firsthand when I represented the Government of Jamaica through its national road company, National Road Operating and Constructing Company Limited, in the restructuring of a concession project to build one of Jamaica's most ambitious toll roads. The North South Highway, as it was called, was granted to CHEC after another foreign party abandoned the concession.

I also represented SIPC and the International Petroleum Company of India's subsidiary ONGC Videsh Limited (ONGC) in their joint acquisition of Omimex Resources, a company domiciled in the U.S. with large upstream and midstream crude oil operations in Colombia.

The Omimex project was a straightforward acquisition with an interesting twist: Omimex conducted a private bid process for the sale transaction. With intense competition during the final stage of bidding among the final three bidders, SIPC (China) joined forces with one of the other shortlisted parties, ONGC (India). At the time, this was one of Colombia's largest energy transactions with foreign capital. The combined business culture of Chinese and Indian national oil companies made for an interesting transaction process. This was one of the earlier major outbound merger and acquisition (M&A) transactions for both SIPC and ONGC, and so the contract negotiations, including post-closing netting issues, were protracted, but it was a successful transaction for all parties on all accounts.

Did you know?

From the sound of it, you might assume that infrastructure finance is a lot of conference calls and meetings, and you'd be right. But sometimes these meetings could be a bit high octane. The due diligence phase of this Colombian transaction had the potential for excitement as we were required to accompany our clients to meetings in Bogota, as well as make site visits to oil-drilling operations in the Magdalena Valley. Colombia was still rather high-risk at the time, and so we were accompanied by armed guards wherever we went. We traveled in bulletproof SUVs and were assured that the glass was indeed bulletproof. Our driver explained this while pointing at a crack in the glass near my head where a bullet had previously tried to enter. Our Colombian hosts were worried for our safety on the site visit, and so actually retained paramilitary guards to look after us on our visit to the Magdalena Valley. Thankfully, the day was rather uneventful. We took a charter flight to a private airstrip near the Omimex upstream operation, which also involved a boat ride across the Magdalena River, and observed a bunch of drilling rigs in action. We also inspected parts of the oil pipeline that the company owned, and saw where local farmers would remove pieces of copper from the pipeline for personal use, which was a risk we identified in due diligence. Fortunately, in the end, that was about as dicey as it got—no sightings of insurgents or guerrilla fighters.

A Level Playing Field?

China's use of the EPC+F model of infrastructure financing—which we will learn more about in the next chapter—has led to the completion of some immense transactions. While this model has provided a basis for China ODI growth and growth in the host countries of the project one has to question whether all of these projects have produced healthy growth. As we have seen multiple times now in the growth of infrastructure finance on the global stage: it follows a virtuous cycle (see Chapter 12) where it evolves new methods which are sometimes beneficial but often times they test the market and produce negative by-products.

Indeed, China's growth internationally through ODI has not been without its criticism from the international community. In particular, China has found itself on the wrong side of what has grown into the G20 Principles of Quality Infrastructure Investment (QII Principles). The QII Principles[15] place a heavy emphasis on private capital solutions; sustainable, resilient, and environmentally friendly development and connectivity; measuring the life-cycle costs of all infrastructure projects; social inclusion; and the importance of infrastructure governance. Many Chinese ODI projects, some of which are high-profile, have been cited for lack of conformance with these sacrosanct rules of sound infrastructure development and financing. Issues identified by various reports have included the improper siting or oversizing of infrastructure projects, opacity in procurement practices, debt sustainability, and debt transparency.[16] The Chinese ODI model and their practices will require substantial reforms before neutral observers deem them to be in line with international norms such as the QII Principles.

---

15 G20 Principles for Quality Infrastructure Investment, https://www.mof. go.jp/english/policy/international_policy/convention/g20/annex6_1.pdf.

16 See Council on Foreign Relations Independent Task Force Report No. 79, "China's Belt and Road: Implications for the United States," March 2021, https://www. cgdev.org/sites/default/files/how-china-lends-rare-look-100-debt-contracts-foreign-governments.pdf; and Anna Gelpern,Sebastian Horn, Scott Morris, Brad Parks, and Christoph Trebesch, "How China Lends: A Rare Look Into 100 Debt Contracts With Foreign Governments," a report of Aid Data, Kiel Institute for the World Economy, Center for Global Development and Peterson Insitute for International Economics, March 2021, https://www.cgdev.org/sites/default/files/how-china-lends-rare-look-100-debt-contracts-foreign-governments.pdf.

CHAPTER 10

THE WHALES SET SAIL

By Seth Tan

n the aftermath of every crisis—financial or otherwise—new giants emerge. This was certainly the case after the Global Financial Crisis of 2008.

What started off as a good idea of helping more people own homes in the U.S. turned into a subprime crisis that rapidly and adversely affected the rest of the world. It was a reminder that the world was intricately linked with the U.S. financial ecosystem. The lower documentation requirements for home loan applications, together with easier liquidity from mortgage-backed securities rated by top credit rating agencies, increased the risk of moral hazard in the market.

Like many others, I became a casualty of the crisis. I lost my job as the parent company (Babcock & Brown) of the Asian infrastructure fund that I was helping to set up collapsed. With not many new job opportunities in sight, many peers decided to hunker down to wait out the financial tsunami. One decided to take a yearlong caravan trip around Australia with his young family. Others stayed on remote islands in Asia to minimize expenditure. Prompted perhaps by midlife crisis and also a desire for further adventures, I decided to take up a new job in Beijing to work for an African bank (Standard Bank) to bring to Chinese entities opportunities in Africa, Russia, etc.

The Financial Crisis created a vacuum in the international infrastructure market—many infrastructure giants were badly affected. Furthermore, China had already completed most of its in-country developments and urbanization projects so there was relatively less domestic activity. As a result, many Chinese companies were ready to venture overseas with their strong track record and a huge workforce in building infrastructure. China's GDP had grown from around US$1 trillion in the late '90s to around US$5 trillion in the late 2000s. Chinese entities were consequently very much sought after in emerging markets as everyone knew China now had the financial firepower to deploy into large projects.

Engineering, Procurement, and Construction Plus Financing—Oh My!

Supporting some of the top Chinese enterprises and banks, I ended up traveling more and meeting more government ministers than in any other period of my career. Even when I was not accompanying top management of Chinese companies and banks, some of the emerging market governments' ministers and senior officials were still keen to meet me to learn more about accessing Chinese financing. The need for me to travel to Africa (from Beijing) was so large that even when the Icelandic volcano eruptions affected air travel for a few months in 2010, I still had to travel to Africa using a south-south route, flying first from Beijing to Singapore, then to South Africa, and then to the country I was visiting.

Even though these Africa trips preceded the formal launch of China's One Belt One Road (OBOR) initiative (later renamed Belt and Road Initiative, or BRI), some of the approaches that the Chinese state-owned companies favored were emerging.

One such approach was a commercial structure called "EPC+F", where a Chinese engineering, procurement and construction (EPC) contractor would propose to undertake the construction of very large basic infrastructure like power projects, ports, roads, railways, airports, mine processing plants, etc., in emerging countries on turnkey contracts. In essence, the EPC contractor was in charge of everything relating to the project and would hand over the keys to the country's government when the project was completed.

To pay for the EPC works, the host country would need to provide a guarantee (often by the ministry of finance) to Sinosure, China's export credit agency (ECA). Sinosure would, in turn, provide up to 95% political and commercial risk coverage to enable financing of up to 15 years from Chinese commercial banks. The structure seemed elegant. The host government often only needed to put up cash of around 15% of the EPC contract value, and that was all that was needed to get a large infrastructure implemented.

This structure looked similar to the ECA financing models from other developed economies that have been prevalent for decades. However, there were a few important differences that resulted in mixed results for the Chinese companies' EPC+F model.

First, there were often no developer nor long-term investor in the Chinese projects. It was dependent on the host government to find ways to check the design, construction, commissioning, and operation of the infrastructure. The problem was that some emerging countries' governments lack the capacity to do so. Many host governments also did not have the financial resources to engage experienced international consultants to assist them in the review and checks.

Second, many Chinese banks were new to these emerging countries, and vice versa. More than one time I had to roll out a map to pinpoint to my Chinese counterparts some of the cities that they were invited by emerging market governments to consider funding for projects. Hence, although the Chinese banks would be the logical parties to check on the project outcomes for the next 15 years, at that time, some of them were not yet fully equipped to do so. Given the asymmetrical financial strength between China and the emerging country, and the host country's reliance on China for many matters, it was not hard to imagine that banks relied more on the host country's guarantee than the project's performance.

Thirdly, the EPC contractors themselves were also often not undertaking the same projects that they implemented in China, which had moved on to the next level of development—more advanced infrastructure technologies and renewable energies.

On the other side of the globe they were needed to install more basic infrastructure like roads or the previous generation of power technology. I was involved in a power project for an emerging country where the EPC contractor had to arrange for the equipment to be custom-made because it was no longer manufactured in China

Hit or Miss

Against this backdrop, the risk of moral hazard increased for some projects using the EPC+F structure. Even for very credible state-owned enterprise groups, some projects that were implemented had dismal results. One much talked about example was the "Crash Programme" in Indonesia. As Indonesia was in severe shortage of electricity to support its growth, the government agreed to let several Chinese EPC contractors build large-scale power projects in the late 2000s using the EPC+F model. However, many of the projects completed did not generate the level of electricity that were advertised.

Another example was the Morupule B power project in Botswana. In 2010, Botswana imported 80% of its electricity from neighboring South Africa, and the government's own experience was only that of a small 33 MW coal-fired power project using pulverized coal boiler technology. Consequently, when the government embarked on building a more advanced 600 MW Moruple B coal-fired power project using a different technology (circulating fluidized bed, or CFB), its team did not have the experience to check on the details of such a large power station using this newer technology. The Chinese EPC contractor that won the project on the back of a very competitive EPC price also did not have a strong track record in implementing projects using the new technology. Shortly after installation, problems started to occur in some of the boiler units.

To make matters more complicated, oftentimes in emerging markets, the implementation team representing the two sides did not share a common language, so they had to use two interpreters.

There were instances I observed personally where lengthy negotiations would drag on only for someone to realize that it was a moot point based on a mistranslation because one or both of the interpreters were not technically proficient.

鸡同鸭讲 *A Duck Talking to a Chicken: Lost in Translation*

To be fair to the Chinese banks, they did conduct due diligence with the support of specialists—like technical, financial, and legal consultants. However, the level of details consultants offer is inevitably less than what project owners would do. In the case of the Morupule B project, there was also an African development bank and a multilateral development bank involved in the financing as well, but the technical issues still occurred. It should be noted that there were many projects using the EPC+F model that succeeded. But unfortunately, the projects like some of those in the Indonesia "Crash Programme" and also in high-profile cases like Morupule B caught the attention of many.

Even though it was a structure that could be replicated in many markets, the EPC+F models did not consistently deliver sustainable infrastructure, and in fact, delivered some well-known failures. Much like what happened in the U.S. subprime crisis, the lack of checks and balances increased moral hazard. With money signs in their eyes, some people took advantage of the market to make quick returns at the expense of the long term. Others, on the other hand, did not even manage to make quick returns because they won the project but weren't even able to complete it.

Regardless, this period of time showed once and for all that Chinese companies were becoming giants across all sectors. They were everywhere I went—Ghana, Zambia, UAE, Siberia and even near the border of Brazil, to name a few—helping to advance a significant amount of infrastructure and also causing a sea change in the global infrastructure scene. Around the same time, another whale-like change was happening in the energy market in the U.S., which also had significant impacts on the infrastructure world: renewables.

CHAPTER 11

THE CHANGING LANDSCAPE OF U.S. ENERGY

By Mitchell A. Silk

While China experienced significant infrastructure growth both domestically and internationally, I returned to the U.S. in 2005 to find that the U.S. was taking energy independence and infrastructure growth to a new level. In what perhaps can be seen as an end goal of infrastructure finance, the U.S. had remarkably achieved energy independence through technological innovation in the exploration and production of shale gas and the rapid growth of renewable energy development and finance. Concurrently, the U.S. energy and infrastructure finance markets grew to meet the tremendous capital needs of this period through the rise of private investment funds focused on energy and infrastructure.

These developments, combined with a renewed focus on carbon reduction, led to the intensified focus on transitional energy and infrastructure that is the topic *du jour*. That is, once U.S. market participants felt confident enough with the present and near future, they set their sights on the future. These giant shifts significantly impacted the nature of my practice. My work in Asia had focused predominantly on long lead project structuring, development, and financing work for sponsors and financiers. This experience certainly served me well in my transition back to the U.S. in assisting clients in some of the giant solar projects and infrastructure fund formations of the period.

These market trends also shifted my plate of work to higher speed and higher velocity mergers and acquisitions, as well as complex exercises to structure, form, and close on investor commitments in large infrastructure funds.

The Game Changer of U.S. Energy Independence[17]

The first key factor behind the change in landscape was the U.S. shale revolution. The U.S. achieved energy independence literally overnight with technological advancements in horizontal fracturing technology that gave rise to the shale gas and shale oil explosion.

U.S. oil production reached

14 MILLION

barrels/day in 2014, an extraordinary increase of

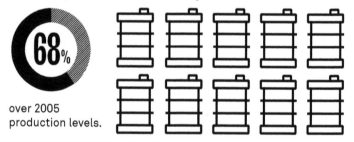

68%

over 2005
production levels.

Similarly, US natural gas production soared to

31,895 BILLION

77%

cubic feet

over 2005 levels.

---

17 For a fuller discussion, see "The Changing Landscape of the U.S. Energy Market U.S. Shale Gas Developments: Investment Opportunities from the Wellhead to the Burner Tip," Allen & Overy Thought Leadership Series, (Summer 2011), 22 pp. (booklet with Paul Mohler, Gary Lazarus and Rebecca Perkins), reprinted as "US shale changes the game," Project Finance International, Issue 456," (May 5, 2011), pp. 42-47 "The Changing Landscape of the U.S. Energy Market-Natural Gas-Fired Electric Power Plants: A Key Element For Future U.S. Energy Policy," Allen & Overy Thought Leadership Series, (Summer 2011), 19 pp. (with Paul Mohler, Gary Lazarus and Noah Baer).

By 2015, the U.S. had overtaken Russia and Saudi Arabia as the world's largest producer of petroleum and natural gas hydrocarbons. In the same year, the U.S. shifted from being a net importer to a net exporter of hydrocarbons.

This advent gave rise to a flurry of transactional activity, ranging from sales and acquisitions of upstream leasehold rights, investment in drilling operations, mid-stream production or export facilities, gathering and processing transactions, investments in pipeline infrastructure, and the development of projects involving numerous downstream applications, most notably power generation. The nature of my worked shifted from the typical plate of drafting and negotiating project documents for sponsors and working on large project financings to mergers and acquisitions that were the transactional means of transferring value of developers of upstream rights to financial investors, like the infrastructure funds discussed below sitting on large pools of not-so-patient capital. Many owners of upstream rights that had successfully tapped into commercially viable shale reserves were selling down positions in their fields. The transactional cycle and cadence was much quicker than the large project financings that I had worked on until this point, with deals completing in two to three months, as opposed to two to three years.

The newfound U.S. energy independence meant that U.S. energy supply factored significantly into global energy security issues, adding novel and interesting policy and political dimensions into the space. In addition, a rapid build-out of U.S. oil and gas midstream infrastructure took on a new sense of urgency and importance. Interlinkages with foreign energy markets, particularly in Asia but also Europe and Latin America, required a rapid-response ramp-up to liquefied natural gas (LNG) export terminal capacity to allow U.S. energy producers to claim their place as a critical part of the global energy economic value chain. Out of this emerged several significant players engaged in the development and financing of mega-projects involving the construction and operation of LNG export facilities and innovative gas marketing and sales strategies to provide long-term stable cash flows to support the export facilities, and a heightened level of challenging transactional and financing activity.

These LNG export facilities—known as midstream infrastructure—were and still are the giants of global energy markets since they are the critical link between upstream producers/sellers and downstream users. These are the type of projects that provide the greatest intellectual charge and practical fulfillment to an advisor and financier interested in global growth. The challenge of the exercise is solving for equitable risk allocation of the midstream terminal while also factoring into account the massive commercial, financial, operational, and technical risks presented by the upstream and downstream projects inextricably linked to the midstream terminal. One terminal implicates billions of dollars of capital investment, hundreds of thousands of jobs, and meaningful energy access for millions. I spent two years grappling with these challenges in connection with one of Taiwan's largest proposed LNG receiving terminals. In addition, a number of these LNG terminal projects factored heavily in my work at U.S. Treasury in countries like Panama, Jamaica, Colombia, Argentina, Brazil, and Vietnam.

Growth of Energy and Infrastructure Funds

Related to, but also wholly separate from, U.S. energy independence, the U.S. asset management markets spawned a new and vibrant investment strategy in the "real assets" space in the form of private equity-style energy and infrastructure funds. This class of funds was a natural extension of many major houses' real estate fund offerings given that real estate and energy and infrastructure development and finance share many common structures and financing approaches, and because all energy and infrastructure projects are anchored by real estate. The rapid growth of the U.S. energy markets up and down the economic value chain described immediately above generated very significant capital needs. This new breed of real asset fund stepped in to meet the capital gap. The practical implications on transactional activity were that brownfield mergers and acquisitions (M&A) surged and many professional service providers went from being limited recourse project finance experts to experts in multi-jurisdictional fund structuring and formation and M&A transactions. In just over a decade, unlisted infrastructure fund assets under management had grown to over US$325 billion by 2015, having started off in the single digits in the early 2000s.

Source: Preqin Pro, "Global Infrastructure Report," 2020.

This represented a new importance that institutional investors placed on energy and infrastructure as an asset class. The growth of energy and infrastructure funds is of immense importance from a markets standpoint since these funds provided the first channel for large pools of institutional investors (like pension funds, insurance companies, foundations, and sovereign wealth funds) to increase their miniscule exposure in this asset class. Over half of these assets were focused on investments in North America during this period, though growth of energy and infrastructure funds pursuing investment strategies in emerging markets has been and continues to be on the rise.

The asset managers during this period were merely following the money and were heavily focused on opportunities in the oil and gas sector flowing out of the U.S.'s newly gained energy independence, as well as growth in other quadrants of the infrastructure sector. For example, as a reflection of the relative size of the market at the time, a new breed of clean energy funds took root during this period.

The oil and gas-oriented funds were chasing deals up and down the energy value chain—upstream companies in distress, companies chasing the wealth of opportunities in the rapidly expanding area of pipelines and transmission networks in desperate need of upgrade and expansion, oilfield services companies, and power generation companies. Most of the notable asset management platforms raised funds to capitalize on investment opportunities in North America's oil and gas industry with total commitments of each fund typically north of US$1 billion, and many of the funds way north of that amount with some exceeding US$4 billion and a few even more than that. These fund sponsors included Blackstone, Warburg Pincus, Carlyle, and Apollo. There were, of course, many more, including infrastructure funds of a more general nature by leading asset management platforms including Macquarie, Global Infrastructure Partners, Brookfield, JPMorgan Asset Management, EIG Global Energy Partners, ArcLight Capital Parners, Antin Infrastructure Partners, Morgan Stanley, Ardian, Goldman Sachs, Blackrock, KKR, EQT, and Stonepeak Infrastructure Partners.

These new capital players concluded some of the largest energy and infrastructure transactions in the market, including: EIG Global Energy Partners investing US$1 billion in Breitburn Energy Partners LP, a publicly traded oil and gas exploration and production company, Quantum Energy Partners investing US$1 billion in Linn Energy LLC to fund acquisition and development of oil and natural gas assets and Riverstone Holdings and Apollo Global Management's US$7.2 billion acquisition of EP Energy, an exploration and production company focused on shale assets. Importantly, many of these funds were the financial partners behind growth and expansion of LNG midstream expansion, especially export terminal, that were so integral to the maintenance of U.S. energy independence.

During this period, I worked on a number of fund launches in the space for leading sponsors like JPMorgan Asset Management, as well as anchor investments by large institutional investors, including international pension funds, insurance companies, and sovereign wealth funds, into some of these funds. My plate of M&A transactions into energy assets, including portfolios of gas-fired and renewables projects, on behalf of fund purchasers increased significantly. Work during the first half of my career was focused mainly on structuring the contours of a project for equity investors developing greenfield projects, or representing the lenders to projects of the type that I was assisting clients develop. With the advent of energy and infrastructure funds, a new class of financial investors emerged in the energy and infrastructure space. This new class of investors required lawyers who understood the intricacies of structuring and forming collective investment vehicles that met the needs of large institutional investors, with all of their complex tax and regulatory needs, disclosing the risks associated with investment in energy and infrastructure projects and being able to execute on purchase or sale transactions of completed energy or infrastructure assets.

A fund formation exercise could take anywhere from nine to twelve months to complete in the good case. But when done, the fund sponsor would essentially have a war chest with which it would invest in brownfield projects available in the market. My earlier work as a project sponsor lawyer gave me valuable tools for understanding project risks and disclosing those risks appropriately in disclosure documents used in fund marketing. I was also well versed in conducting legal and commercial diligence and risk analysis on brownfield assets already in commercial operation on a highly effective and expeditious basis once the fund was up and running and actually investing in projects. I assisted clients in forming a number of funds that pursued investment strategies in general infrastructure, as well as more exotic strategies like distressed precious metals mining projects, shipping and related logistics, and renewable and clean energy.

Renewables Take Off

Concurrent with the shale revolution, renewable energy experienced hyper-growth, globally and particularly in the U.S, brought about by two significant factors. First, solar installation costs began to drop materially in the early 2010s. Advances in technology reached grid parity by the mid-2010s even without government incentives. Specifically, there was a marked drop in distributed solar PV system prices by 12-19% in 2013, resulting in installations costs of more than 50% below 2010 prices.

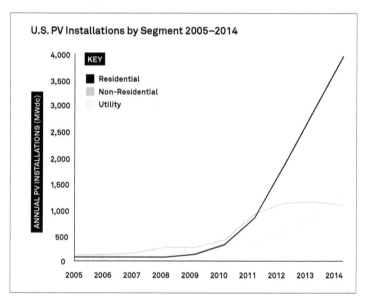

Source: SEIA. Solar Market Insight, 2015, Q4.

Second, a number of Federal and state policy and legal reforms greatly supported the growth of solar energy in the U.S.

These included generous Federal tax credits and local tax incentives, the authorization of US$4 billion in low-cost loans under the Department of Energy Loan Guarantee Program and the adoption of Renewable Portfolio Standards ("RPS") in more than half the states in the U.S. The significance of the growing adoption of RPS was that most states in the country agreed to a time-linked adoption of renewable power production over fossil fuels. As a result, the growth trajectory for solar PV energy in the U.S. was nothing short of astounding. Over 35% of all new U.S. electric capacity in 2014 was from solar, representing approximately 4,000 MW of new production capacity with a new solar project installed every 3 minutes.

The high velocity of renewable project development and finance activity resulted in a requisite increase in the number of specialist financiers and professional advisors, as well as immense capital demand to fuel growth in the field. In addition to a need for experts in tax equity transactions, the burgeoning field also required expertise in a host of other specialties relevant to scaling procurement, construction strategies, and finance. Sponsors required a number of new structures to achieve financial efficiency, many of which revolve around holding company structures that aggregate multiple projects.

My renewables experience was varied and exciting. I worked on a number of utility-scale solar projects throughout the Americas, Europe, and Asia. I was able to utilize the many years of developer experience I had with project documents to successfully close a number of solar and wind projects, including the then largest utility-scale solar project that utilized project bonds for financing in the U.S., and solar projects in Puerto Rico, Hawaii, and Panama. In addition, I worked on a number of complex portfolio financings of solar projects throughout the world, as well as the financing structure to support an innovative platform to support the financing of residential solar assets throughout the United States. The business has grown into one of the largest residential solar financing platforms in the United States that was recently successfully listed as the part of a special purpose acquisition company (SPAC) transaction.

It was interesting to compare and contrast experience that I gained in project development in emerging markets like China to the skills required for the success of a project in a very mature market like the U.S. Success in an emerging transaction requires the highest degree of technical, commercial, and legal knowledge to structure and document a suite of project documents that achieve equitable risk allocation and contain terms that will provide a legal basis for a base case of economic benefits for the investors. Navigating that maze requires a considerable amount of time and resources analyzing the risks and addressing those risks typically through some form of credit enhancement.

Mt. Signal

In a very stable and predictable market like the U.S., political risks are largely not present and the exercise is more that of applying laser focus toward optimizing project delivery and operations and containing costs. By way of example, around 2008, a leading international independent power developer and longtime client from China, AES Corporation, asked our U.S. team to assist with a series of solar projects that they were pursuing in the U.S. through a subsidiary, AES Solar. Benefitting from the experience of my partners in Europe, who were assisting AES Solar on a number of solar projects in Europe, we took the existing European project contract forms and adapted them for the U.S. market, law, and practice. On this basis, we pursued a number of projects for AES Solar throughout the U.S. and North America, ranging from Puerto Rico, to Hawaii, to one of the then largest solar projects in the U.S.—the Mt. Signal Project in California.

The Mt. Signal Project was exciting and exhilarating from the beginning. The AES Project Manager, Tim Montgomery, applied an extraordinary degree of innovation and discipline in the contracting phase of this project that provided the foundation for one of the most successful utility-scale solar projects in the U.S. At every major level of procurement and contracting, Tim scaled and leveraged AES's buying power—fairly and equitably—in an appropriately aggressive and disciplined manner. This approach produced much needed cost efficiencies so important to the competitive and margin-thin U.S. market. His approach was one I had observed in a few of my successful clients in China like Jim Wood, whom I mention in Chapter 7. In addition, his skill in construction contract implementation delivered the success of the project being delivered on time and to budget. This project was by all measures "mean and lean"—far from the "hogs" described in Chapter 7. It was a great lesson on how to implement a successful project.

The Mt. Signal Project has grown into one of the largest utility-scale solar projects in the world, presently at 800 MW. We provided a great base to this extraordinary development. The initial phase that I worked on provides electricity to nearly 75,000 households in Southern California. The plant design enables it to displace over 350,000 metric tons of carbon dioxide per year, roughly the same level of carbon displacement as 15 million trees. That's what I call a good and healthy energy project worthy of pride. A giant project with giant benefits to the world. I recall making the drive from San Diego to Calexico for the groundbreaking ceremony at the site. It was two hours from San Diego to Calexico through ranges of yellow boulder formations followed by a long stretch of desert.

I remember thinking how my work in power had come full circle from my first baseload power project near China's Gobi Desert. The drive from Lanzhou to Jingyuan through ranges of barren and dry mountains bordering the Gobi Desert was very similar in some ways. My first project utilized basic coal-fired steam generation technology and now I was working on a baseload power project in the U.S. that was powered by the most sophisticated renewable power production technologies of the time. I had come full circle.

As I watched the ribbon-cutting ceremony take place at the giant complex, I remember thinking that the solar and renewable revolution had finally arrived; I was officially living in the future, a completely different time from when I had started my work in energy. Across the ocean, China was not far behind and quickly becoming the largest solar market in the world. In the next chapter, Seth will use his experiences in China to illustrate how a huge market potential drives the virtuous cycle of innovation.

CHAPTER 12

THE BIGGER
THE BETTER

By Seth Tan

The bigger the better...or, in the case of my China experience, a bigger market not only offered many more possibilities, but it also contributed to improving the market.

Between 2011 and 2018, China's GDP grew from US$6 trillion to around US$14 trillion. Mirroring the changes Mitch observed in the U.S. in the previous chapter, during this same time period, China's solar power market grew more than five times and made it the largest solar market in the world. This immense growth in various sectors had a deep impact on many areas of the market. Not only were there many opportunities in the China hinterland, but many countries sought Chinese investments or financing into their countries' infrastructure. For international banks, this presented many "inbound" and "outbound" opportunities. Even though all 400+ international banks added up to account for only less than 2% of the domestic lending market, the sizable market was still a big draw.

Like many, I took up the challenge and flew up and down China, fighting "tooth and nail" for each good opportunity. For those among us who were frequent fliers, they would know that it was not easy to achieve platinum level just flying short trips on economy class, but I achieved that for several years just flying within China. To support the frantic flying by bankers and businessmen, Chinese airlines significantly increased flight frequencies. However, airport runways in big cities like Beijing were not sufficient to cope with the increased traffic, hence I would often get onto a plane, finish watching a movie on my iPad, and still be on the tarmac.

Disrupt, Adapt, Grow, Repeat

One phenomenon I witnessed during this time was how some segments of the market became super-competitive. When competition gets intense, so does adaptation. This back and forth creates a virtuous cycle where everyone is putting their best foot forward and trying to outdo one another. It makes for an exciting and fast-moving environment.

The most extreme example happened online. E-commerce became institutionalized during this period and it transformed how sellers reached their customers. As compared to the traditional model of selling to one's neighborhood, for e-commerce, anyone in the 1.3 billion population could be a customer. Interestingly, as customers could openly compare products, it very quickly pushed sellers up the quality curve, both in terms of goods quality and also quality of service. Sellers who received good reviews on the e-commerce app from their customers further positioned themselves to sell more to the market.

The e-commerce boom created a new infrastructure asset class for international investors—ambient warehouses. As the e-commerce market became a giant, giant companies like JD and Alibaba invested heavily to ensure timely deliveries of even very small packages to faraway locations. Logistics warehouses in good locations employing modern equipment that can quickly move goods in, repackage them into the right combination for each customer, and quickly move the goods out, became critical in this nationwide logistics web. This new infrastructure asset class attracted many world-renowned institutional investors.

Interestingly, the intense competition caused by e-commerce in the retail market did not completely collapse the traditional brick-and-mortar retail business. It instead forced businesses to innovate, and the best players found a way to work symbiotically with the online enemy, and even make it a friend.

One of the sectors I covered in DBS China was commercial real estate (or we can call it retail infrastructure) and I had the opportunity to visit many retail malls all around China. Even in cities where there were too many retail malls, the best of them were still the attraction of the city and made a good profit, whilst the retail mall just across the road from them had little or no business. A big feature in some of these winners was the use of data analytics and digital tools. Data analytics allowed very detailed optimization of store mix in the mall, store placement to optimize overall mall foot traffic, and even ways to help individual stores improve sales. Digital tools, on the other hand, which could expand online sales and extend the reach of the mall, could in some cases be used to remember the customers' past mall behavior to better serve customers when they next visit and even prompt more impulse purchases by customers.

So, in a gigantic market, intense competition may not be a bad thing. It can prompt innovation, and that can result in a virtuous cycle. This modern logistics web also improved resilience, and that became very important during the COVID-19 pandemic when some supply chains were affected.

Dog Eat Dog World

Offline, the competition to service quality Chinese corporates (particularly the state-owned enterprises, or SOEs) was also intense. It was not unusual to have over 30 world-class competitors pitching for transactions. When I moved from Asia to Australia in 2003, I thought that was intense competition as often there were close to 20 competitors. China from 2011 took my experience to the next level. I once went to pitch to an SOE and found myself queueing up once I exited the lift. There was a long queue of bankers in the corridor, like we were all going to see a doctor. When it was our turn to pitch, the client still had the pitchbooks of the previous bank opened in front of them. It was a surreal experience.

The fact that everyone targeted the same quality companies meant that the companies received a lot of information. It was not hard to imagine that if a company had over 30-40 banks pitched to them on any matter, the company would become a subject matter expert very quickly. The asymmetry on information was so great that on several occasions I was even asked what was my "proposal's value add compared to another competitor's." It was not just a pure price fight (or price comparison) but could also be on very detailed matters which impacted deliverability and outcomes. Relationship (关系) and being able to survive through dinners involving 50% alcohol content rice wine (白酒) became less important in those super-competitive segments of the market.

Strangely, many bankers (including myself) pushed on despite the intense competition. The possibilities from such a big market were just too tempting. If one missed an opportunity, there was a next one...and next one...and next one. It was almost addictive dancing with the new giants.

To access the large possibilities, many like me have to be constantly on the road. I recall a period of close to nine months I was away from my wife and toddler daughter and, I became a "WeChat father" (微信爸爸). The WeChat video call father figure became so real to my toddler daughter that once she tried to share with me a slice of apple by shafting it to her mum's iPhone. To be honest, I was far from alone in this experience. Every Chinese New Year, over 400 million people in China crisscrossed the country to go back home for a few days, and for many of them, that was their annual opportunity to see their family.

Being away from families is a negative in a very large market. There are however many positives due to the market size. One important positive is innovation.

Solar Nova

A good example of where a massive market made for a virtuous cycle occurred in the solar power sector. Given the potential for technology improvement across the entire solar manufacturing value chain, the Chinese government employed a "carrots-and-sticks" approach, which brought forth huge solar power developments whilst at the same time significantly reducing solar power tariffs for new batches of projects.

China's massive solar market was further underpinned by key enablers like ensuring solar power generated will be taken by the grid (priority of dispatch) and approving each project's tariff for 20 years. All of these elements created a virtuous effect where many enterprises sent their A-Team to this market. This influx of motivated and experienced stakeholders accelerated innovation which consequently reduced the capital costs for newer solar power projects.

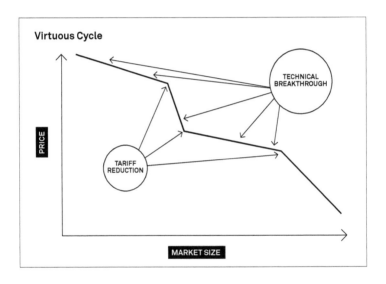

The Chinese government added urgency to acceleration when they signaled when 20-year tariff for new batches of projects would be reduced. The end result was a dramatic drop of solar power tariff from RMB0.95/kWh to RMB0.50/kWh for Class I sites (where solar irradiation was stronger). As China became the largest solar power market in the world, the players who were successful there could also be relevant in other markets, hence it indirectly resulted in solar power tariffs coming down in other countries as well.

As the Chinese solar power market evolved very rapidly in such a short time, there would inevitably be problem pockets. Transmission grid companies needed to play catchup to ensure curtailment went down rather than up. With the increase of intermittent energy generation, the transmission grid also needed to be augmented to ensure the grid could take on the huge amount of solar power. Efforts had to be made to ensure that businesses, industries, and the general public could enjoy uninterrupted power. Due to the looming threat of a lowered tariff, there were issues with some individual projects being sub-optimal. Much like we saw in Chapter 8, in the rush to deploy projects before the 20-year tariff next came down, some projects were not properly prepared and built. But, on the whole, the bigger market and the opportunity for a series of transactions catalyzed a virtuous cycle.

The need for infrastructure will forever remain, but the type of infrastructure needed will change with the needs in that season. The right conditions will result in new giants, which will in turn shape the future.

CONCLUSION
A LOOK TO THE FUTURE

nfrastructure projects have giant timelines. They take a long time to build, a long time to get running, a long time to fund, and we want them to operate for giant periods of decades. The reality of combining giant timelines with the efficiencies and benefits of the innovative and disruptive technology that drives growth in the space means that some of the technology will invariably become outdated or obsolete in the course of the project

These days, technology and other disruptors are introducing impactful products and investment approaches to work toward the immense capital demands of acute transitional infrastructure needs. Therefore, in closing, we'd like to explore what the future of infrastructure and infrastructure finance might look like. How do we prepare for that future together? How do we stay resilient in the face of what will certainly be an increasingly innovative future where new inventions constantly change the way we do business?

Change Is the Only Constant

Society will always need energy and infrastructure. That will never change, but we can be sure that everything else will. Societal needs and circumstances change—sometimes overnight, as we saw during the COVID-19 pandemic. The way energy and infrastructure are delivered and managed can and will change overnight as well. Practically, this means that we must constantly be assessing the market and working "as a team" to adapt our ways of doing business. The findings of those frequent reviews should trigger thinking on how we can and need to adapt to ever-changing market circumstances.

Infrastructure enables innovation and innovation allows infrastructure to adapt and catch up. While this dynamic will not change, we see several lessons from the past—many of which we have discussed in this book—as timeless and paramount. Some of these lessons include better preparation, governments engaging in market sounding with private sector participants, and trying to put in place the enabling environment and commercial structures that is "just-right" while not creating moral hazard. As with everything else, agility and versatility are central in responding to change. The more markets and market participants are agile and versatile in embracing and responding to change, the smoother and more efficient change will be.

Private or Public?

Policy, law, and regulation are inextricably linked with transactional activity and the markets, both of which inform and feed on the other. A good government official seeking to make policy for healthy and impactful infrastructure growth will need to understand the nuances and complexity of transactions and how the markets actually work. Similarly, a good developer and banker must understand the nuances and complexity of policy and regulations in order to fashion good deals. Investors and their advisors would do well to encourage their star team members to serve in government, and similarly governments need to arrange more practical secondments along the lines of the U.S. Department of State's Lawrence S. Eagleburger Fellowship Program. This excellent program details mid- to senior-rank diplomats to leading corporates and financial institutions to provide career U.S. diplomats with firsthand business and commercial knowledge through hands-on training in the private sector.

For emerging markets in Asia, Latin America, and Africa, the level of private sector involvement is very low. Hence, finding ways to get private sector involved and invested in infrastructure would help with accelerating growth and bringing newer ideas.

Governments can help create the enabling environment to attract international private sector into their countries' infrastructure needs. Growth will come quicker and more effectively when policy moves in tandem with transactions in the field.

The more that policymakers can factor in private sector needs and concerns through, for example, private sector soundings and advisory groups, the more the policymakers will have their fingers on the pulse of what the market requires. Similarly, the more sensitive and aware the private sector is to prevailing and developing policy, the easier it will be for them to calibrate activities to policy and regulation.

All of the greatest growth policies in the world will not necessarily get developers and investors to the table if they don't know about the opportunities that new policy, regulation, and programming are designed to bring about. That's why it's important for governments to highlight and publicize important policies and programming to ensure a high level of awareness among those who might benefit and participate. Therefore, strategic communications and investor/private sector roundtables are vital.

The public and private sectors need each other to be successful in infrastructure. It is not an "us *versus* them" situation; it is an "us *and* them" partnership. One of the government's responsibilities is to ensure there are sufficient checks and balances during the planning, design, construction, operation, and maintenance phases of energy and infrastructure projects. At the same time, governments must be adept and vigilant in incorporating ongoing ideas from private sector so the needs of the times are properly addressed. This can be very important during wartime or a global pandemic, for example, when we need to ensure logistics workers and truck drivers can continue to be mobilized despite lockdowns. Another example could be the government allowing the conversion of office buildings to mixed-use buildings as more people work from home. With the greater availability of technology, data, and digital tools (including digital twins—a digital version of the proposed/actual infrastructure to allow running of what-if scenarios in a dynamic way), it is possible to plan for more "buffers" without necessarily increasing the cost exponentially.

As situations change quickly, all stakeholders need to come together to reorganize infrastructure to address society's current needs. In this way, government and private sector are two sides of the infrastructure coin.

Slow Down in Order to Speed Up

Infrastructure development and finance is not for the impatient. The reality is that all energy and infrastructure projects have a long lead to establish a project concept, conduct early development, design and engineer the project, actually build and commission the project, not to mention financing the project. In a good case, the process might not be less than 18 months, but, in most instances, it's longer.

Rushing rarely pays off, quite the opposite actually. We have found that taking the appropriate time in planning to pinpoint value pools and look at the market holistically will slow progress but yield efficiencies later in the process. There is a frequent need to slow down in order to speed up. With that said, there are a few great and specific ways for policy makers to ensure effective, efficient, and impactful infrastructure policy and program planning:

1) Needs Not Wants:

One way to ensure time is spent wisely is to focus on needs rather than wants. We've seen cities and governments waste months exploring projects which they really want but which a preliminary review would have shown is not sustainable or needed. While we of course all want the shiny new energy or infrastructure technology, it's important to start from the bottom up, understand the real needs in the round and ensure that program and project framing address holistic needs in the round and make good economic and technological sense.

2) Friends in All the Right Places:

It's vital to have the right collaborators. Willing government counterparts and the right mix of funding and technical partners on the project side are key to move forward projects through all their phases. For newer infrastructure for emerging markets, the right "anchors" supporting and pushing it forward are of paramount importance.

3) For Everything There Is a Season:

When a country needs power to support its development, it is imperative to focus on developing power projects or re-powering existing projects to increase their sustainability. When a country needs to improve its trade connectivity, logistics and supply chain projects become important. In emerging markets throughout the world, it is also important to ensure projects are developed more quickly as the season could come to an abrupt end of a political cycle with new focus after elections and after new office holders come into place. This may be one of the reasons why some infrastructure projects start well but do not move forward well—their origination cycle was too long and anchor stakeholders moved on. Fortunately, the market learns from each project.

Carbon Reduction

Over the past few decades, we have seen a massive growth in demand for all types of conventional infrastructure, including transmission and interconnection, gas-fired power, transportation, and logistics. This includes everything from baseload power to surface transportation; from seaports to airports; and from freight and passenger rail to water treatment and supply facilities. Today, our environmental response—colloquially known as sustainability—has in many ways overtaken growth requirements from conventional areas. Specifically, transitional infrastructure has become a priority. In this area we are thinking of value-add renewable energy (conventional renewables with some element of technological value add, like solar plus storage); digital infrastructure, distributed energy (like micro- and mini-grids); energy efficiency projects of all sorts (such as multimodal municipal street lighting projects and energy efficiency building refurbishment projects); and transportation decarbonization. We see electric power transmission and distribution as an area that is grossly overlooked. It was underdeveloped prior to the advent of transitional infrastructure, and transitional infrastructure is now creating an even higher and more critical demand for rapid growth in this area.

Due to these reasons and many more, infrastructure that helps with decarbonization, and environmental adaptation and mitigation has and will become increasingly important and popular. These are, however, not easy problems to solve. For example, we used to design infrastructure that could withstand rainfall that has a probability of occurring once in one hundred years. Durable design of course adds to the cost of the infrastructure. Today, we are faced with the fact that the supposedly "once in a hundred years' rainfall" now happens every few years. Hence, all stakeholders may need to be prepared to come together and adjust accordingly, even for infrastructure that has already been built.

Transitional Energy and Infrastructure

Most of the change in the U.S. energy market, and elsewhere throughout the world, stems from the rise of *transitional* energy and infrastructure—energy and infrastructure projects that will enable the world to transition to growth in energy and infrastructure with a materially lower carbon footprint through technological innovation. Growth and developments in this field have been as rapid and impactful as the shale gas revolution and the renewables revolution that followed. This new area of energy and infrastructure has emerged through a number of market trends.

First, the increased focus on decarbonization combined with distributed energy innovation have been key drivers. In particular, policies across the globe focused on decarbonization, decentralization, and energy access are driving unprecedented demand for renewable energy, transmission and distribution infrastructure, decarbonized transport, and energy efficiency. Capital demand for growth in this area is projected to be not less than US$1 trillion a year through 2030, some put the estimate much higher. Second, digital connectivity has become a basic necessity, and is essential to global economic growth. Global data flows have grown over 45x over the past decade, accounting for a 10% increase in world GDP. In addition, expansive industrial internet and new digital grid growth are critical to stability and resilience for global economies. Third, markets and stakeholders demand Environmental, Social and Governance (ESG) accountability. As such, ESG accountability has become an essential and integral pillar in setting corporate business strategy and defining responsible business practices. These are three market trends that are and will continue to shape the contours of investment in energy and infrastructure for the coming decade.

The last decade has indeed seen profound changes in the landscape of energy and infrastructure globally, with consequential impacts on how transactions in the sector are structured and financed. The markets have grown and become increasingly diversified, as have the financial tools and financing structures. This growth in market diversity resulted in the constant change and challenge that ensured that work was always highly interesting and rewarding. We now must fasten our seatbelts as we confront the giant growth to come in these new areas of transitional energy and infrastructure that builds on many of the traditional structures and concepts dealt with in this book, but will also require us to push the limits in project structuring, implementation, and financing in accommodating this new streak of innovation.

At the same time, this giant growth will require giant funding, and public funding is not the solution, and is certainly not sustainable. Given the vast pool of institutional capital available (presently over US$110 trillion), a very low allocation (roughly 1.5%) of this capital to infrastructure, it is imperative that private capital mobilization is at the center of meeting these giant capital needs. Attracting private capital providers will require hard work and innovation to create new markets and broader channels for meaningful increases in private capital investment while decarbonizing, enhancing access, and lowering costs to realize sustainable development. In addition, these challenges require comprehensive solutions that leverage the combined resources, collective efforts, and effective partnerships among all key stakeholders, including public sector, private capital participants (including institutional investors, banks, corporates, impact investors, and infrastructure funds), as well as governments and donors. Finally, success requires holistic programming with targeted priorities. This must include establishing priorities for target regions and sectors, and pursuing growth through scale, leverage, and uniformity of approach in the framing, development, documentation, and financing of projects.

In Closing

Our friendship started on a competitive note and ended on a collegial one. After over 20 years pursuing our respective careers in the private sector dancing with giants, we both ended up serving our respective governments by using infrastructure finance tools to further our respective governments' national interests. At the sidelines of the first formal U.S. Government to Singapore Government bilateral meeting, we realized that despite our separate journeys, we ended up with very similar views on how to scale up infrastructure development and finance.

The world is at a critical turning point in confronting acute needs for financing the infrastructure needed to support global growth. This increased challenge results from the astronomically large size of the global infrastructure funding gap measured at not less than US$1 trillion a year, the impact of COVID-19, and a renewed focus on decarbonization, transitional energy, and digitalization.

For those aspiring participants in the field of infrastructure finance, we would like to encourage your participation sooner rather than later. Infrastructure will play a pivotal role in the future, and taking a deal from concept through development, construction, operations, and finance is fulfilling and intellectually rewarding. Beyond that, it is on us to bring about the giant growth and assist in meeting the giant capital demands. And, certainly, giant challenges are the precursors to giant rewards. We both are very pleased with our career choice. Indeed, our career choice has yielded tons of fond, meaningful, and even humorous memories, and allowed us to contribute tangibly toward shaping a brighter future.

Thank you for reading.

About the Authors

Mitchell A. Silk

Mitchell is the immediate past Assistant Secretary for International Markets at the U.S. Department of the Treasury. Mitch designed an inter-agency growth initiative that assists partners of the United States unleash value in their energy and infrastructure sectors by identifying impactful and scaled investment opportunities that rely on private capital solutions. He also designed and implemented the $94 billion CARES Act programs that benefitted over 700,000 American aviation industry workers, played a senior role in the trade negotiations with China and reform, oversight of OPIC and the Export–Import Bank of the United States, and the establishment of U.S. International Development Finance Corporation.

During his 30 year legal career, 20 of which he spent as partner of the global elite law practice Allen & Overy, Mitch developed deep expertise in real assets matters (including energy, infrastructure, mining, and real estate), asset management, banking and finance, and legal matters in China and Asia, as well as growth capital matters involving technology with disruptive applications in energy and infrastructure.

Mitch is fluent in Mandarin and Cantonese Chinese, and his favorite language of Yiddish. He lives in Brooklyn, New York. He and his wife, Yocheved Rivka, are the proud parents of eight children and four grandchildren.

Seth Tan

Seth was most recently the head of Infrastructure Asia, a regional infrastructure facilitation office under the Singapore government. Initiatives he led include bringing top private sector companies to co-create bankable Asian infrastructure and standardizing a portion of project finance documentation to help reduce time and cost to close transactions. Seth has worked in the infrastructure sector for 25 years, across a broad spectrum of infrastructure and over a large geographical area (even economies further away from Asia like Zambia, Nigeria, and Ghana). Thanks to esteemed employers like BNP Paribas, Babcock and Brown, Standard Bank, and DBS Bank, Seth worked outside Singapore for 15 years and traveled to almost 80 cities across the globe.

His favorite cities are Beijing (where he lived for 9 years) and Singapore (home). He now lives in Singapore with his wife, Li Xiang, and their children, Zoey and Evan.

Mitch's Acknowledgments

My views set out in this short—and what is meant to be fun—volume were informed by the exceptional colleagues, clients, and counterparts with whom I was blessed over my 30-year legal career and more than three years in the U.S. Government. My acknowledgments and warmest thanks go to friends and former colleagues at:

Coudert Brothers, a law practice that no longer exists in name, but continues on in spirit, where I first cut my teeth on the challenges and rewards of project finance with mentors Peter D. Cleary, Owen Nee, Lucille Barale, and Thomas E. Jones.

Chadbourne & Parke (now known as Norton Rose Fulbright), and, particularly, my mentor and supervising partner, the legendary project finance practitioner Rigdon Boykin and the great team that staffed its Hong Kong office.

Allen & Overy, the global law practice where I spent 20 years and where I learned so much about energy and infrastructure finance from some of the greatest legends in the field, in particular, at the risk of overlooking some, and in no particular order other than periods that we worked together: Paul Monk, Jonathan Brayne, Graham Vinter, Anne Baldock, David Morley, Philip Wood, Sidney Myers, Thomas E.W. Brown, Chris Rushton, Thomas E. Jones, Mark Sterling, Alan Rae-Smith, Simon Black, Kenneth Chan, Cathy Yeung, Roger Lui, Vicki Liu, Matthias Voss, Victor Ho, Jane Jiang, David Wainer, Andrew Ballheimer, Wim Dejonghe, Jay Pultman, Matt Huggett, Pamela Chepiga, Andrew Rhys-Davies, Gareth Price, Kent Rowey, Robert Kartheiser, Cathleen McLaughlin, Bruno Soares, and Etay Katz. And a special thanks to the team that I built: Jillian Ashley, Mingzhang Zeng, Victoria Guo, and Niso Matari, as well as Olivia Cheung, my executive assistant for a number of years, first at Chadbourne and later at A&O, and Carrie Ng, who ably followed Olivia in Hong Kong, and Dawn France-Somersol and Roselyn Montero in New York;

The U.S. Department of the Treasury, where serving as Assistant Secretary for International Markets was the most rewarding position of my whole career. This position provided a base to pursue my passion to close the massive global infrastructure funding gap through my work to create a new inter-agency growth initiative in energy and infrastructure finance. I designed this program to further U.S. interests abroad by assisting U.S. partners unleash value in their energy and infrastructure sectors by identifying impactful and scaled investment opportunities that rely on private capital solutions. My immense thanks to our leadership for supporting this work: Secretary Steven T. Mnuchin, Deputy Secretary Justin Muzinich, David R. Malpass (former Under Secretary of International Affairs and now President of the World Bank), Heath Tarbert (my former law partner at Allen & Overy, former Assistant Secretary of International Markets at Treasury and former Chairman of the Commodities and Futures Trading Commission), Adam Lerrick (former Counselor to the Secretary), Brent McIntosh (former Under Secretary of International Affairs), Mauricio Claver-Carone (former Special Assistant to the President and Senior Director of the United States National Security Council's Western Hemisphere Affairs Directorate, former Treasury colleague and present President, Inter-American Development Bank), Sigal Mandelker (former Under Secretary for Terrorism and Financial Intelligence), David F. Eisner (former Assistant Secretary for Management), Thomas Feddo (former Assistant Secretary for Investment Security), Geoffrey Okamoto (former Acting Assistant Secretary for International Finance and Development and present First Deputy Managing Director of the International Monetary Fund), J. Steven Dowd (Immediate Past U.S. Executive

Director, European Bank of Reconstruction and Development and African Development Bank), DJ Nordquist (Immediate Past U.S. Executive Director, World Bank), Eliot Pedrosa (Immediate Paste U.S. Executive Director, Inter-American Development Bank), Mark Rosen (former U.S. Executive Director to the International Monetary Fund, and Jason Chung (Immediate Past U.S. Executive Director, Asian Development Bank). And tremendous gratitude to Eli Miller, Baylor Myers, and Zac McEntee, as well as my front office of Daniel S. Katz, who provided very sound counsel and showed extraordinary dedication, Talia Rubin, who kept the trains moving.

Thanks also to many good friends and partners at other key agencies for their leadership in deploying my programming that involved using the tools of infrastructure finance to further U.S. national interests, including Adam Boehler (former U.S. International Development Finance Corporation Chief Executive Officer), D.J. Gribbin (former Special Assistant to the President for Infrastructure), John Rader (former Deputy Assistant to the President and Advisor for Policy and Strategy), Thomas Storch (former Deputy Director, National Economic Council and former Deputy Assistant to the President for International Economic Affairs), Timothy Fitzgerald (former Chief International Economist, Council of Economic Advisors), Kimberly Reed and David Slade (former Chairman and President and former General Counsel, respectively, Export Import Bank of the United States), Keith J. Krach (former Under Secretary of State for Economic Growth, Energy and the Environment), Frank Fannon (former Assistant Secretary of State for Energy Resources), Steven E. Winberg (former Assistant Secretary of Energy for Fossil Energy), Bonnie Glick (former Deputy Administrator for the U.S. Agency for International Development), Joseph Semsar (former Acting Under Secretary of Commerce for International Trade), and Thomas R. Hardy (former Acting Director, U.S. Trade and Development Agency).

My U.S Government infrastructure finance program operated

through the efforts of hundreds of extraordinarily dedicated and talented officials at the Department of the Treasury, including virtually all of the exceptional Deputy Assistant Secretaries in International Affairs, my fantastic team in the office of Investment, Energy and Infrastructure led by Devesh Ashra, Lida Fitts, and Victoria Gunderson, as well as colleagues in Washington, D.C., and our missions abroad of the Department of State, the U.S. Agency for International Development, and the U.S. Trade and Development Agency, Department of Commerce, Department of Energy, Department of Transportation, the U.S. International Development Finance Corporation, and U.S. Exim Bank. Thank you all!

Special thanks to Jared Kushner, Ambassador David Friedman, Jason Greenblatt, Avi Berkowitz, and Aryeh Lightstone for allowing me to apply my infrastructure finance programming approach to their very important and successful work in the Middle East.

During my government service, I served as Head of the U.S. Delegation to the G20 Infrastructure Working Group. This work provided an exceptional opportunity to consider solutions to the global infrastructure funding gap alongside critical thinkers from so many great key partners, and contributed to my thinking on issues in the Conclusion. Thanks to Argentina, Japan, Saudi Arabia, and Italy for your exceptional leadership, and to friends in Australia, Singapore, the United Kingdom, Germany, and beyond!

And, finally, my infrastructure finance programming benefitted greatly from our partners in the 20 governments with which the U.S. Government signed bilateral frameworks and another 20 governments with which we had informal programming. The partner countries covered by the program's frameworks are:

In Latin America and the Caribbean, Argentina, Bolivia, Brazil, Chile, Colombia, Dominican Republic, Ecuador, El Salvador, Guyana, Haiti, Honduras, Jamaica, and Panama, and in Asia-Pacific, Japan, South Korea, Singapore, Taiwan, Vietnam, Indonesia, and Thailand.

In addition, the program extended to other countries through ad hoc work not covered by formal frameworks. These countries include Mexico, Guatemala, Peru, Suriname, Paraguay, Uruguay, Trinidad and Tobago and a number of other Caribbean countries, China, India, Bangladesh, the Philippines, Malaysia, Laos, Saudi Arabia, the UAE, Israel, Egypt, Jordan, Papau New Guinea, the Solomon Islands and the Marshall Islands.

My thanks to the Finance and other ministry colleagues in all of these countries for informing my thinking and working with us to make the world a better place through infrastructure finance. Seth was one of my key interlocutors in this work, and I am indebted to him for being such a great partner and friend.

Dear friends Avrumie Sieger and Naftuli Brachfeld have provided their very kind support to this work.

I have always been blessed with great friends and clients (some beginning as the former and some as the latter, all forever friends) who have greatly benefitted my work detailed in this book, including Isser Elishis, Christopher P. Reynolds, James Wood, Paul Freedman, Ashley Wilkins, Yoshihiro Megata, Steven Greenspan, Neil Auerbach, Junyuan Gu, and Ed Kania, and all of whom have taught me a lifetime of knowledge about the various topics covered in this book.

Our warm thanks to those who kindly endorsed this book.

And the best for last—my family. None of this would have been remotely possible without my dear wife Yocheved Rivka (Chevie), the kids (Meshulam (and Noga), Bella, Malka Aydel (and Meyer), Moishe Yitzchok (and Dina), Chavie, Naftuli Chaim, Mordechai Dov and Taube Raitze (Toby)), and the grandchildren (Toyvia Boruch, Raizel, Yitzchok Tzvi and Meshulam Zusha), and the tremendous support, bountiful happiness, and sense of purpose and mission that they provide.

All thoughts, views, and faults are my own.

Seth's Acknowledgments

I hope everyone had fun reading this short book, and for those who took the same or similar journeys, I hope our stories prompted nostalgia for all the fun (and not so fun but very memorable) moments in their infrastructure journeys. My own journey would not have been possible without the support and trust of many bosses, clients, partners, and collaborators. Just in the last three years at Infrastructure Asia, I had the support of many leaders (in fact giants) from close to 600 entities, and it would be impossible to acknowledge everyone. For my acknowledgments, I look back on the last two plus decades and acknowledge those who gave me a chance to dance with the giants.

First, I would like to acknowledge my wife, LI Xiang, my daughter, Zoey, and son, Evan. Many of us in the same shoes would know that it would not have been possible for us to spend so much time and be on the road so much if our families were not supportive.

I would like to thank the companies I worked for. Without the trust of BNP Paribas, Babcock and Brown, Standard Bank, DBS, and the Singapore government, I would not have such a rich infrastructure journey across many sectors and countries.

At BNP Paribas, I would like to thank Christophe Rousseau, Robert Dolk, Christopher Thieme (who is now at the Asian Development Bank), Bruce Weller, Prema Balakrishnan, and Shalen Shivpuri. I had a story about Christophe that did not make it to the final book, but suffice it to say he was the first project finance giant I encountered in my career.

At Babcock and Brown, my kudos to Warren Murphy and Raymond Fung who showed me the science and art of infrastructure. Their analysis on renewables like wind certainly even impressed technical consultants who were supposed to be specialists at wind power.

At Standard Bank, I would like to acknowledge Craig Bond and Jonathan Wood, who showed me that with ingenuity and tenacity it was possible to finance infrastructure even in frontier markets.

At DBS Bank, I would like to thank Tan Teck Long and Adrian Chai for entrusting me with not just developing business in the energy sector, but also logistics, retail and healthcare sectors, and also the five teams (particularly the team heads George Wang, Jennifer Xiao, Claudia Ning, Andrew Tang, Jacky Yeung, and also Freya Deng) who supported me in delivering some very interesting and landmark solutions to clients. This era certainly enriched my experiences as I learnt how to dance with giants in these sectors and learnt from top clients how they survived and thrived in a very competitive China environment through innovation, using data and digital tools, etc.

At Singapore government, I would like to extend a special thanks to Minister Indranee Rajah, who gave me the runway to establish the platform to help more Singapore-based private sector investors and solution providers into Asian infrastructure. Special thanks also to the entire infrastructure Asia team (past and present) and in particular Kow Juan Tiang, as together we started to show it is possible for government and private sector to come together to co-create to make more infrastructure happen.

As I said in one of the chapters, the era makes the hero. One thing I noticed in over two decades in infrastructure is there are indeed many "heroes" who seized the moment, and created a difference. One of them is Mitch Silk (my co-author for this book). Kudos to him for synthesizing all the learnings and experience to help more private sector win in infrastructure in his public service role. Two clients from very different sectors also come to mind, one is State Grid of China (particularly Li Hong) and the other is Shenzhen-headquartered retail group SCPG (particularly Li Chu Hua). They were both very large groups and yet managed to challenge themselves to embrace innovation. There are others I met who worked hard to do things differently, do things better, and make a difference, like Keiko Honda who led MIGA of World Bank Group to more than double their political risk insurance coverage to infrastructure during her tenure; Marie Lam-Frendo for her continuous efforts to highlight on a world stage the importance of infrastructure and how to make infrastructure better; Lim Chze Cheen who worked tirelessly to show how a regional organization like ASEAN could make a difference in regional connectivity; Wong Heang Fine and Pang Yee Ean who showed that a professional services group from a small country like Singapore could be a world leader in its field; and Nicholas Wong (Clifford Chance) and Kok Chee Wai (Allen & Gledhill) who believe it is possible to standardize a portion of project finance documentation and thereby accelerate the market. I would like to recognize these individuals and many more not only for making infrastructure projects happen, but for showing it's possible to make our world better.

We both offer our greatest gratitude to Raab & Co. who helped edit, design, produce, and publish this book in record time, specifically editor Josh Raab, designer Andrew Bell, proofreader Farah Ameen, cartoonist Jon Klassen, and e-book producer Kim Peticolas.

Image Credits:
p. 16, Will Burgess; p. 24, Seth Tan; p. 32, Al Simonov; p. 42, Robin T W Henderson; p. 48, HelloRF Zcool; p. 56, Seth Tan; p. 62, Tina Lorien; p. 70, WDG Photo; p. 76, MicroStockHub; p. 88, Nico Faramaz; p. 96, bauhaus1000; p. 108, Seth Tan. Cartoons on pages 23, 26, 36, 65, 83, 93 by Jon Klassen.